THE BRITISH LIBRARY
HISTORIC LIVES

Winston Churchill

THE BRITISH LIBRARY
HISTORIC LIVES

Winston Churchill

Stuart Ball

NEW YORK UNIVERSITY PRESS
Washington Square, New York

Cover illustration: Winston Churchill, 1941, in Ottawa to address the Canadian Parliament regarding defence.
Yousef Karsh/Camera Press Ltd

Half-title page illustration: Churchill as Privy Councillor, 1915.
Henry Guttmann/Getty Images

Title-page illustration: Churchill with Field Marshal Montgomery (on his left) in Germany, 7 March 1945.
Fred Ramage/Getty Images

First published in 2003 by
The British Library
96 Euston Road
London NW1 2DB

Designed and typeset
by Andrew Barron @ thextension

Printed in Hong Kong
by South Sea International Press

First published in the U.S.A.
in 2003 by
NEW YORK UNIVERSITY PRESS
Washington Square, New York
www.nyupress.org

Text © Stuart Ball 2003
Illustrations © The British Library
Board and other named copyright
holders 2003

Library of Congress Cataloging-in-
Publication Data
Ball, Stuart, 1956-
Winston Churchill/Stuart Ball
p. cm. – (The British Library
historic lives)
Includes bibliographical references
and index
ISBN 0-8147-9919-1 (alk. paper)
1. Churchill, Winston, Sir, 1874-
1965. 2. Prime ministers-Great
Britain-Biography. 3. Great Britain-
Politics and government-20th
century. I. Title. II. Series.

DA566.9.C5B25 2003
941.084′092-dc21 2003054006
[B]

Contents

Making a mark 1874–1904

Winston Spencer Churchill's family background was aristocratic, political and slightly disreputable. It fostered his sense of history, but also contributed to the egotism which marked his career. Winston was born on 30 November 1874 at Blenheim Palace, the grand mansion in Oxfordshire built by John Churchill, the first Duke of Marlborough, in the early eighteenth century and named after the greatest of his victories against the French. His military and political skills had elevated the Churchills to the heights of the peerage, but to many of the aristocratic families whose lineage went back to the Norman Conquest they remained brash newcomers.

Whilst the heroic figure of the first duke provided the backdrop, the most crucial influences on Winston were his parents – especially his father, Lord Randolph Churchill. The latter was the younger son of the 7th Duke, and so would not inherit the family title or land. In February 1874 he became the Conservative Member of Parliament for Woodstock, the small borough near Blenheim in which the family influence was strong. In April of the same year Lord Randolph married the heiress and beauty Jennie Jerome. She was the eldest of the three daughters of Leonard Jerome, a wealthy New York stockbrocker who was then living in Paris. Such unions between new American wealth and British aristocrats whose estates needed an infusion of cash were a feature of the period, but one which attracted criticism. Winston's trans-Atlantic parentage was another key element in his background, encouraging his democratic instincts and the importance of a 'special relationship' with the United States – of which he was a living embodiment.

Winston was born only seven months after his parents' marriage – he was either two months premature, or had been conceived out of wedlock. A younger brother, John (always known as 'Jack'), was born in 1880, but there were to be no

Previous page: Churchill in the full
dress uniform of his cavalry regiment,
the 4th (Queen's Own) Hussars, in
1896, shortly before being posted
to India.
Getty Images

other children. Lord and Lady Randolph cut striking figures at the forefront of
London society, moving in the fastest and most fashionable circles. However, in
1876 Lord Randolph was involved in a dispute over gambling with the Prince
of Wales (Queen Victoria's eldest son, who became King Edward VII in 1901),
and the Churchills withdrew to Dublin until matters cooled. Here he acted as
personal secretary to his father, who had recently been appointed Viceroy of
Ireland by the Conservative government. Lord Randolph acquired a close
knowledge of Irish affairs which was to prove valuable as his political interests
developed, for the 'Irish question' – the problem of how Ireland, with its majority
Roman Catholic population, should be governed – became central in British
politics from the 1880s to the First World War.

The return to office of the Liberals under Gladstone in 1880, and the
disarray of the Conservative leadership after the death of Disraeli a year later, gave
Lord Randolph an opportunity. He rapidly emerged from the backbenches as the
most effective critic and talented speaker on the Conservative side. He exploited
the Liberal government's embarrassments and weaknesses, and at the same
time treated with disdain the staid and moderate Conservative leader in the
Commons, Sir Stafford Northcote. So independent were Lord Randolph and the
two or three MPs who acted with him that they became known as the 'Fourth
Party' (the others being the Liberals, the Conservatives and the new party of Irish
'Home Rulers'). Lord Randolph was a sharp and witty debater, but he also made
his mark as a new kind of popular politician – he was closer in style to Joseph
Chamberlain, the radical Liberal, than to most conventional Conservatives.

The 1880s were a decade of political change, with the rise of platform
speaking at public meetings, a growing press and a substantial increase in the
electorate due to the Third Reform Act of 1884–85. Lord Randolph's political

career became an enduring myth, as his meteoric rise was followed by catastrophic downfall, wretched illness and early death. He was brilliant, cynical, passionate, opportunistic, unpredictable and egocentric; one of the outstanding and fascinating personalities of the age, he made the political weather in the 1880s. Populist and demagogic, Lord Randolph evoked the 'Tory Democracy' of Disraeli, although he was no clearer about what this meant in practice. Gladstone's proposal to concede Irish Home Rule – the establishment of a parliament in Dublin to deal with most internal Irish affairs – led to a convulsive political crisis in 1885–86 which split the Liberal party and resulted in twenty years of Conservative dominance. Lord Randolph played a key role, and was rewarded with the position of Chancellor of the Exchequer in Lord Salisbury's ministry in July 1886.

The political world seemed to be at Lord Randolph's feet, but misjudgement and arrogance led to a fatal miscalculation. He sought to outdo the Liberals in economising on spending, antagonised his colleagues and, in January

A letter written by Winston, aged 6, to his mother; although he often signalled his affection, his parents were remote and unresponsive. *The British Library, Add. MS 45850, f.1–1v*

My dear mama I am so glad you are coming to see us I had such a nice

1887, threatened resignation in an attempt to coerce the Prime Minister. Glad to dispense with a troublesome minister and potential rival, Salisbury took the offer at face value and swiftly accepted it. The government was barely shaken, but Lord Randolph's political position was destroyed and he was never to recover. At first, he was simply erratic and embittered, but it became clear that he was suffering from a far more serious problem. Within a few years he had passed into the twilight, as his strength and powers ebbed. He became a pathetic figure: halting, rambling, and suffering from embarrassing lapses of memory in public. His decline was thought to have been due to syphilis, a disease which evoked scandal as well as horror, but it has more recently been suggested that he had a brain tumour. Neither illness was treatable in those days, and Lord Randolph died in January 1895, at the age of forty-five.

Lord Randolph's legacy to his son was more than just a famous name and useful contacts. It was the cause of Winston's fascination with the world of high politics and his desire to follow in his father's footsteps. There was also a sense of promise unfulfilled, of insecurity and the pressure of time, which particularly affected Winston's career in his early years. He suffered much hurt and feelings of rejection from his father's distant and dismissive attitude, but responded with even greater love and uncritical hero-worship. One result of this was a lifelong fidelity to the myth of 'Tory Democracy' which enabled Winston to be flexible and sometimes radical in his views. There were also negative aspects – many looked for, and found, evidence of similar instabilities in Winston's character, and

bathe in the
sea to day.
love to papa
your loving
winston

predicted his breakdown. Churchill's desire to seek the limelight, to be noticed and regarded, were present throughout his life, and clearly relate to the emotional deprivation of his early years. He also came from a class which still saw their role as being the natural governors, and that is what Churchill most wanted to do. The periods which he later spent out of power were neither natural nor comfortable for him; he sometimes flailed wildly in his attempts to escape from them, with unfortunate results.

Churchill's early years coincided with the peak of Britain's power in the world. The first nation to industrialize, it was still at the centre of trade, banking and shipping. The world's largest navy ruled the waves with the sublime confidence of Nelson's heirs, protecting the routes which linked the largest empire ever seen. During his short career as a cabinet minister, Lord Randolph had strengthened Britain's hold over the Indian sub-continent with the annexation of Burma in 1885. As well as the 'jewel in the crown', India, there were the developing Dominions of Canada, Australia and New Zealand, and a string of strategic islands and ports including Gibraltar, Malta, the Cape of Good Hope, Singapore and Hong Kong. In 1882 Egypt was occupied, and by the end of the century the 'scramble for Africa' had left Britain with the lion's share, making possible the dream of a Cape-to-Cairo railway running solely through British territory. In 1878 the Conservative Prime Minister Benjamin Disraeli forced Russia to back down at the Congress of Berlin, and twenty years later his

Opposite: Winston (right), aged 14, with his mother and younger brother, Jack, in 1889; 'she shone for me like the evening star', he later wrote.
Getty Images

successor Lord Salisbury needed no allies when confronting France over the control of the Nile Valley in the Fashoda crisis of 1898.

Pride in British achievements and power, the grandeur and romance of the far-flung empire, and the moral certainty which accompanied them, all profoundly influenced the young Churchill. Belief in Britain's world role and historic destiny remained with him throughout his life, and was central to his outlook. It was both a weakness and a strength, making him seem unwilling to consider reform in India in the 1930s and encouraging attempts at an influence beyond Britain's capacity after 1945. At times he seemed to be part of another world, and almost a ridiculous figure. However, this was also the foundation of his confidence and pugnacity in 1940, the two qualities which his sincerity and power of language enabled him to convey to the nation and the world at the most critical stage of the Second World War. It was on the foundation of these late-Victorian certainties that in those dark days he became the voice and focus of national determination and resilience.

Churchill's career was built on foundations which he crafted for himself as a young man, for his childhood and schooling were difficult and unproductive years. They were marred by the distance of his parents – preoccupied with their own social and political interests – and then by the tragedy of his father's decline. The most constant and loving presence in his early years was his nanny, Mrs Everest. She gave him the physical affection and emotional security which he lacked from his parents, and Winston remained in close contact until her death when he was twenty. The love which he repeatedly signalled to his father was met only by neglect and disappointment, and in his early years his elegant and fascinating mother was almost as remote. 'She shone for me like the evening star', he wrote in *My Early Life*, which was published in 1930; 'I loved her dearly – but

at a distance.' Matters were made worse by Winston's failure to come up to parental expectations at school, either in the classroom or on the playing fields.

Boys of his social class were usually educated at boarding schools from an early age. Bullying, brutality, homesickness and loneliness were the common lot, but certainly Winston's experience seems to have been more miserable than most. The worst came first: in 1881, at the age of seven, he was despatched to St George's School at Ascot, not far from London in Berkshire. He spent three unhappy years in its harsh regime, suffering from the endemic bullying, until the severity of the headmaster's beatings – considered excessive even for those days – led his mother to remove him. In 1884 he went instead to the gentler atmosphere of a school in Hove, near Brighton on the Sussex coast, run by two maiden sisters, the Misses Thomson. These 'preparatory' schools were the common route to 'public' school, the establishments where the wealthy elite sent their sons. Eton and Harrow were regarded as the two most important of these, and Winston attended the latter from April 1888 to December 1892. He was considered a frail child, and was prone to catching colds. He nearly died during a serious bout of pneumonia in March 1886, and so Harrow's airier location was considered by his parents to be the safer option.

Opposite: Churchill's commission
as a 2nd Lieutenant in 1895.
The document is signed by Sir Henry
Campbell-Bannerman, Secretary of
State for War in the 1892–95 Liberal
government; in 1905, as Prime Minister,
he gave Churchill his first ministerial
appointment.
*Chartwell Trust/Churchill Archives Centre,
CHAR 1/13/1*

He later described the period at Harrow as 'the only barren and unhappy period of my life'. He struggled with the work, and had only one real friend (Jack Milbanke, later killed at Gallipoli). His conduct did not conform to the norms of manliness and modesty, and he suffered from bullying to which he responded with aggressive defiance. Concerned that he was not by instinct physically courageous, he sought to overcome this and raise his prestige with displays of daring and bravery. However, breaking the rules got him into regular scrapes, and his rashness could be dangerous; on one occasion, he ruptured a kidney and was unconscious for three days after jumping off a bridge during a game of 'tag'. Throughout his life he was to seem reckless and impulsive, and the distrust which dogged his political career until 1940 was due to this as much as his unconcealed egotism and ambition. Churchill's slight physique meant that he did not shine at most sports. He was best in individual activities, such as swimming and rifle shooting, and his one distinction at Harrow was winning the public schools' fencing championship in 1892. His schoolwork was not as poor as was sometimes later suggested, but fell far below his father's high expectations of excellence.

It is now considered that dyslexia was the root of Churchill's educational difficulties, but in this era the problem was not understood. As he was clearly an intelligent boy, his teachers and parents assumed that he was not trying hard enough, and responded with hectoring and punishments. Churchill did not shine in any subject, and had particular difficulties with maths and the classics, which were an important part of the syllabus. However, he enjoyed history, which focused upon kings and battles, and gave a generally uncritical view of the rise of British power and stability. He also absorbed English literature and, like many dyslexics, he had a capacious and retentive oral memory; soon after arriving at

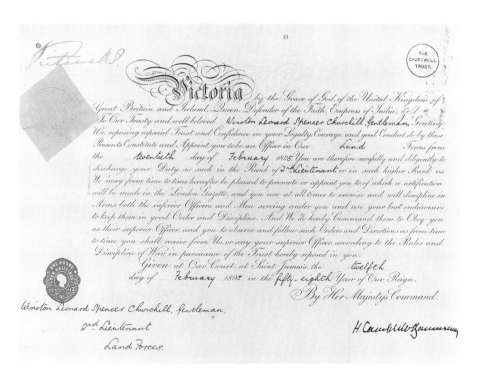

Harrow, he won a prize by reciting 1200 lines of poetry. The ability to quote passages was far more emphasized than it is today and was seen as the natural accomplishment of an educated and cultured mind, and Churchill had an unusual flair for this. He was later to use this skill in preparing his speeches, most of which were memorised before delivery. This increased his confidence and verbal fluency, but it also led to a certain inflexibility.

Winston did not seem to be university material, and as early as 1889 his parents decided that he should aim instead for the Royal Military Academy at Sandhurst and a military career. He needed the help of special tutoring to pass the entrance exam, and secured a cavalry cadetship on his third attempt in 1893. He found the practical nature of the course to be more congenial and passed with credit in December 1894, placed eighth in the class of 150. In February 1895 he joined the 4th Hussars, a fashionable cavalry regiment, as a 2nd Lieutenant. Although his favourite childhood hobby had been commanding huge armies of model soldiers, even before his father's death his ambitions had become focused on politics. The army would be a suitable apprenticeship for a few years, gaining experience before following his father into public life. In August 1895 he told his mother: 'It is a fine game to play – the game of politics – and it is well worth waiting for a good hand before really plunging.' His aim in the next few years was to seek adventure and a chance to distinguish himself. A period of leave in October 1895 was used to obtain his first assignment as a war correspondent, and he heard shots fired in anger for the first time whilst reporting on the conflict between the Spanish colonial authorities and the guerrilla rebels in Cuba. He spent the following year in Britain, striving to be assigned to Egypt or Matabeleland in south Africa, where there was the prospect of action and opportunties to distinguish himself. He had no success, and in September 1896 sailed with his regiment to India. However, he was to see active service on the north-west frontier during a punitive expedition against the Afghan tribes in the autumn of 1897. Although these were skirmishes rather than battles, there was a real danger of being killed and Churchill had some narrow escapes. This campaign became the topic of his first book, *The Story of the Malakand Field Force*, which was published in March 1898.

By this time Churchill was desperate to join the army being assembled to reconquer the Sudan, which had been lost in humiliating circumstances after the death of General Gordon in 1884. He appealed to his mother for help and her charm and social contacts smoothed the way. In July 1898 he was given a temporary attachment as a Lieutenant with the 21st Lancers, and during August he travelled with the expeditionary force up the River Nile. The British forces had the advantages of discipline and superior weapons, and on 2 September routed the main Dervish army at Omdurman, not far from Khartoum. One of the most famous and decisive moments of the battle was charge of the 21st Lancers, in which Churchill took part; this was to be the last major cavalry action of the British army. Two days afterwards he wrote to his mother: 'I was under fire

Kitchener of Khartoum

THE RIVER WAR

AN HISTORICAL ACCOUNT OF

THE RECONQUEST OF THE SOUDAN

BY

WINSTON SPENCER CHURCHILL

AUTHOR OF 'THE STORY OF THE MALAKAND FIELD FORCE, 1897'

EDITED BY COL. F. RHODES, D.S.O.

Illustrated by Angus McNeill, Seaforth Highlanders

IN TWO VOLUMES
VOLUME II.

LONGMANS, GREEN, AND CO.
39 PATERNOSTER ROW, LONDON
NEW YORK AND BOMBAY
1899

all day and rode through the charge. I fired 10 shots with my pistol – all necessary – and just got to the end of it as we cleared the crush.'

During his time in India Churchill embarked on an prodigious programme of reading in preparation for a career in public life, sending his mother lists of the books which he required. This self-instruction was the most important and influential stage of his education, and ranged voraciously across history, literature, philosophy and economics. Churchill discovered that he had a flair for writing which he could use to earn money and gain public recognition. He reported on the Sudan campaign for a London newspaper and afterwards produced a two-volume account, *The River War*. His military histories and journalism were often sharply critical of the higher military and political authorities, and Churchill was becoming a controversial figure – his pulling of strings aroused resentment, and he was seen as a self-publicist and glory-seeker. Wider opportunities beckoned in journalism and politics, and with little regret he resigned from the army on 3 May 1899. He had already spoken at a few political meetings in the autumn of

Previous pages: On attachment in the
Sudan, Churchill took part in the last
great cavalry action of the British army:
the charge of the 21st Lancers in the
battle of Omdurman, 2 September 1898
(litho by Richard Caton Woodville,
1856–1927).
Private Collection/Bridgeman Art Library

1898, having encouraging success and enjoying the experience. In July 1899
he made a first attempt to enter the House of Commons in a by-election at
Oldham. This was a Lancashire industrial town, where his father's memory and
the cry of 'Tory democracy' might cut some ice with the working-class voters.
Churchill threw all his energy into the campaign, addressing packed meetings and
gaining confidence as a public speaker, and was only beaten by a small margin.

Within a few weeks a more serious colonial war had begun in south Africa,
where the semi-independent Boer republics were seeking to prevent British
control of their internal affairs. Churchill secured a lucrative engagement as war
correspondent for the *Morning Post* (the newspaper which had employed him
in the Sudan), and arrived at Cape Town on 31 October 1899. At the start of
the conflict the outnumbered, but more agile, Boers had inflicted a series of
humiliating defeats on British forces, and several towns were now encircled
and besieged. Keen to be at the forefront of the action, Churchill obtained
an invitation to travel on board an armoured train on a reconnaissance mission
into Boer-occupied territory. However, on 15 November the train was ambushed
and derailed, and Churchill was amongst those taken prisoner. He had taken an
active part in defending the train, showing nerve under fire and being mainly
responsible for the escape of the engine. Not surprisingly, the Boers paid little
attention to his claims to be only a journalist, and he was perhaps fortunate
simply to be treated as a prisoner of war and confined with the others in a
former school in the Boer capital, Pretoria. His initial hopes of parole or an
early release were disappointed, and so his thoughts turned to escape. A plan
was hatched with the officer who had commanded the train and an Afrikaans-
speaking sergeant, and Churchill went first over the wall of the school on
12 December. His companions were unable to follow, and later there were

recriminations that he had behaved selfishly and spoiled their chances. In fact, Churchill had taken risks in waiting for as long as possible near the prison, and found himself in a difficult position as he had no food, no map, and could not speak the Boer language. The Boers offered a £25 reward for the recapture of their well-known prisoner 'dead or alive', and Churchill's successful escape was a saga of adventure and lucky chances. He was fortunate to encounter an English-born mine manager who hid him for several days, and he was then concealed on a train which was travelling to the coast through the neutral territory of Portuguese Mozambique.

When Churchill arrived in Durban on 23 December 1899 he was hailed as a war hero, for his audacious escape was one of the few bright spots in a dismal period of British defeats. The affair was given much publicity at home, and made him a well-known figure. He immediately enlisted in a local volunteer unit, the South African Light Horse, but was allowed to continue to report the war as well. He remained in south Africa for the next six months and was often under fire, taking part in the bloody and unsuccessful battle of Spion Kop in January 1900. As the war gradually turned in Britain's favour, he was present at the relief of Ladysmith and the occupation of Pretoria. He returned to England in July and, after being paraded in triumph through the streets, was again adopted as Conservative candidate for Oldham. Soon after, the Conservative government called what became known as the 'khaki election', exploiting the war atmosphere and the divisions in the opposition Liberal Party. The change in popular opinion was enough to give Churchill victory by 222 votes and he was elected to the House of Commons on 1 October 1900, two months before his twenty-sixth birthday. Not one to waste time, he delivered his maiden speech early in the new Parliament on 18 February 1901, rising from his father's old place to urge a firm but generous policy to finish the conflict in south Africa, which was now entering a bitter and costly phase of guerrilla warfare.

Churchill had succeeded in making his name and, almost as importantly, an adequate fortune – for in this era a Member of Parliament received no salary and was expected to have sufficient private means to support himself and mix in upper-class London society. After the election Churchill undertook tiring but lucrative lecture tours in Britain, Canada and the United States, and his despatches from the Boer war were republished as two books. During 1899 and 1900 he earned £10,000 from writing and speaking, a very substantial amount in those days. Invested for him by one of his father's friends, the banker Sir Ernest Cassel, this gave Churchill a steady income and made his political career possible. He was never really wealthy, but was able to add to this foundation with later earnings from journalism and books.

The young Winston made an impact through personality and energy rather than physical presence. He was of slight build and, at 5 feet 6½ inches (169 cm), was below average in height. He had a rounded face, protuberant eyes, high forehead and receding, slightly sandy hair. His youthful countenance was the mirror of his emotions, radiating vigour, enthusiasm, impulsiveness and sometimes mischievousness. He had a slight lisp, which remained with him, and a stammer which he overcame by hard work and willpower when starting out as a public speaker. In 1900 he was captured by the caricaturist 'Spy' in a typical speaking pose with his hands on his hips, at once jaunty and combative. The accompanying commentary was shrewd and prophetic: 'he is ambitious; he means to get on, and he loves his country. But he can hardly be the slave of any Party.' So it was to prove, as Churchill's course during the next forty years cut across conventional party loyalties, a buccaneering progress which left him distrusted on all sides as an opportunist with thoughts only for his own advancement.

In 1900, as one of the youngest MPs and a household name – in his own right, and as his father's son – Churchill seemed ideally placed. The rise of his father's generation to the top of the political ladder in the 1890s meant that the young Winston could look for patronage and support amongst some of the leading figures of the day. His father's unconventional approach had brought him friends and admirers in both parties. These included Conservatives such as Sir Michael Hicks-Beach, the Chancellor of the Exchequer from 1895 to 1902, and prominent Liberals including Lord Rosebery, briefly Prime Minister in 1894–95, and John Morley. Churchill's contacts thus spanned the party divide, reinforcing his own ambivalence. He was already aware that it was mainly loyalty to his father which had led him to seek election as a Conservative – and this was a weak link indeed, given Winston's uncritical view that Lord Randolph had been shabbily treated by the present party leaders, Lord Salisbury and Arthur James Balfour. Lord Randolph's idiosyncratic radicalism was also reflected in his son's outlook, and Winston's first political actions echoed both the start and end of his father's career.

In July 1901 he joined with a few other maverick young Conservative backbenchers in a group strikingly reminiscent of the 'Fourth Party'. They were known as the 'Hughligans' – or more often, 'Hooligans' – after their leading figure, Lord Hugh Cecil, the son of the Prime Minister, Lord Salisbury. Their aim was to cause havoc and enjoy themselves, using obstructionist methods and debating skill, and their fire was frequently directed at their own side. They also had useful social connections, and some of the leading figures of both parties were guests at the group's weekly dinner. Much of this was tolerated by the Conservative leaders as youthful high spirits, but Churchill also opened up another and more serious line of attack on the issue which had led to his father's resignation as Chancellor of the Exchequer: the need for economy in military expenditure. From his first major parliamentary speech in May 1901 – which he spent six weeks preparing and learning by heart – Churchill emerged as a vigorous critic of his own government's proposals for reforming the army. After the failures of the Boer War, no one doubted that reform was urgently needed, but Churchill denounced the schemes as both ineffective and wastefully expensive. These speeches got Churchill noticed, but once again he seemed to be out of sympathy with his own party; as his father had found, calling for cutbacks in defence appealed to Liberals more than Conservatives.

A thorn in the sides of his leaders and unpopular with the mass of loyal backbenchers, Churchill became increasingly uncomfortable as a Conservative MP in 1902. The retirement of the aged Lord Salisbury and the succession of his nephew, Balfour, as Prime Minister in July 1902 made little difference, and Churchill was certainly too young and rebellious to be considered for office. Instead, like others in both parties in these years, he was drawn to the idea of a new centre grouping that would rise above narrow party squabbles; this was all the more attractive as its prospective leader was Lord Rosebery. The prospect of a realignment of parties always appealed to Churchill's desire to shuffle the deck and deal a fresh hand all round, with talent and boldness reaping their just rewards. He dallied with this prospect in 1902–3, but despite his urging Rosebery failed to act. During this period Churchill had also begun to investigate the new area of poverty and social issues at home, and this reinforced his feelings of sympathy for the condition of the poor and his restiveness with Conservative attitudes and measures. He was therefore already semi-detached from his party when the political world was convulsed by the issue which was to dominate most of the next thirty years and cause Churchill's first change of party.

In May 1903 the second most powerful figure in the Conservative cabinet, Joseph Chamberlain, launched a public campaign for 'tariff reform'. This would require a fundamental change in the British economy, as it meant abandoning the free trade system which had been the foundation of Britain's prosperity in the Victorian age. However, the prospect of a rise in the cost of living due to tariffs on imported food was very unpopular in the industrial areas. Chamberlain's initiative completed the revival of the Liberal Party and badly divided the Conservatives. Churchill had immediately emerged as one of the most vigorous defenders of free trade, although it had not been a burning issue with him before. This was an example of his lifelong pattern of forming a view, convincing himself by the vigour of his arguments, and ending up with an extreme and rigid position which he would stubbornly refuse to amend. His assaults on Chamberlain and the party leadership were so vehement that they caused problems for other Conservative free traders, and a gap opened up between them. The leading free traders were mainly of the older generation, including some of Lord Randolph's friends, but they were fading away and gave no effective lead. Between 1903 and 1905 Chamberlain's policy gained ground in the party and the Conservative 'free fooders' became a beleaguered minority. Some compromised, whilst the hard core were driven from their constituencies or into retirement. Churchill was one of the very few who ignored the tug of party solidarity and took the defence of free trade to the logical conclusion of changing party allegiance.

Churchill's adamant opposition to tariff reform broke his remaining ties with the Conservative Party. In January 1904 the official whip (the formal recognition of an MP's party membership) was withdrawn and a vote of no confidence was passed by his constituency association in Oldham, although they

February 2. 1904

105, MOUNT STREET,
W.

Dear Mr. Balfour.

I expressed no desire in my letter of the 22nd to receive the Government whips as you cannot fail to see if you read it through again. I neither invite them nor decline them. As a Unionist Free Trader I am opposed to what is generally known as Home Rule & to Protection in any form. I cannot regard your administration as any satisfactory security against

did not want to force a by-election and were willing for him to remain as MP
until the end of the parliament. Churchill already had contacts amongst the
Liberal leaders, and now entered into closer discussions with them. By April 1904
he had agreed that at the next general election he would stand as a free trade
Liberal in the constituency of Manchester North-West; this contained the
business district of the city most identified with Victorian free trade, and its
capture would be a symbolic victory. The process was completed on 31 May
1904, when he formally crossed the floor of the House of Commons and sat
upon the Liberal benches. This has always been a very unusual and controversial
step, but — although risky — it was not impulsive. It was neither purely the course
of principle (as Churchill naturally maintained) nor of naked opportunism
(as his enemies alleged), but a fusion of the two. Certainly, there was little by
way of conviction, obligation or party loyalty to hold him back. Churchill
had no particular religious feelings and the conflict between Anglicanism and
nonconformity — which for many in both parties was crucial to the distinction
between Conservatives and Liberals — did not engage him. The Balfour
government was visibly crumbling and the Liberal Party had been reinvigorated,
but the Conservatives held onto power for another eighteen months. Churchill's
prospects may have seemed brighter in the Liberal Party, but in May 1904 they
were still recovering from nearly a decade of disarray in opposition; their victory
at the next election seemed likely, but was not assured. Churchill's temperament
was not one of cool calculation, and he was always drawn to the prospect of
action and opportunity; like Blücher at Waterloo, his instinct was always to march
towards the sound of gunfire.

2

Changes of direction 1904–1915

Churchill's change of party proved to be a timely move, for the decade from 1904 to the outbreak of the First World War in 1914 was one of division and defeat for the Conservative Party. However, the Edwardian era saw a triumphant return to power for the Liberals and perhaps their most successful reforming government. No one witnessing the comparative health of the parties in these years could have expected that this would also be the last Liberal government, after which this historic party would decline and nearly disappear. The Liberals' hold on power from 1906 to 1915 reinforced assumptions that Churchill had changed sides to further his ambitions, and added to the bitterness with which Conservatives regarded him. He was reviled as a turncoat and traitor to his class; the lasting resentment remained an important political factor until the end of the First World War, and contributed to his exclusion from office in 1915. The view that Churchill was an unprincipled adventurer was established during this period, and reinforced by later incidents in his career. In the meantime, he incurred some social ostracism and, in some quarters, feelings ran so high that this was even extended to his wife after his marriage in 1908. In just one example, his application for membership of the Hurlingham Club, the exclusive governing body of his favourite sport of polo, was blackballed. However, although he was detested by most of the Conservative rank and file, Churchill retained some friendships across the party divide. The most important of these was with F.E. Smith, who was first elected in 1906 and made his mark with the most audacious maiden speech ever given; they shared a similar outlook and enjoyment of the good things in life, and were often regarded with equal suspicion by the more orthodox and party-minded politicians of both sides.

Since 1902 Churchill had spent much of his time writing the life of his father, and this gave inspiration and justification for his own rift with the Tory

Previous page: Churchill in one of his
typical debating poses; a portrait taken
after he 'crossed the floor' to join the
Liberal Party in 1904.
PA Photos

Opposite: Churchill's life of his father
was a critical and commercial success
when it was published in January 1906,

in the middle of the general election.
The press was important to any
ambitious politician in this era, and
Churchill was swift to forward this
request from the editor of *The Star* to
his publisher, Macmillan (the father
of the later Prime Minister).
*The British Library, Add. MS 55245,
Vol CDLX, f.128*

party. Lord Randolph emerged as an heroic figure, with his inconsistencies
explained away and his democratic impulses emphasised. In presenting his father
as the defender of economy and sound government in 1886, Churchill portrayed
a figure who but for the Irish question could have been – like his son – more
at home in the Liberal ranks. The two-volume work was published on 2 January
1906, in the midst of the general election, and was a commercial and critical
success. During 1904 and 1905 Balfour's Conservative government had slid into
discredit and decay, with its foundations eroded by strife over tariff reform. The
Prime Minister's final desperate throw was to resign office in December 1905
in the hope that the pressure of forming a government would expose Liberal
divisions. This did not happen, and when Sir Henry Campbell-Bannerman
constructed his administration Churchill was offered a junior position in it,
becoming Under-Secretary for the Colonies on 10 December 1905. As the
Liberals were still the minority party in the House of Commons, Campbell-
Bannerman called a general election immediately after forming his government.
Polling began on 12 January 1906; it was not until 1918 that voting was held
everywhere on the same day. The result was a disaster for the Conservatives, as
they lost nearly 250 seats and were reduced to their lowest-ever total of 156 MPs.
The landslide had swept in 400 Liberal MPs and 30 of their junior ally, the
newly-formed Labour Party, and Campbell-Bannerman's government also had
the general support of the 83 Irish Nationalists.

The Liberal success, in which Churchill's victory in Manchester North-
West was a small part, was due to negative fears of 'food taxes' rather than any
positive Liberal programme. It was only later that social reform became an
important factor, and Churchill was to play a significant part in the emergence
of a 'New Liberalism' – more interventionist than the *laissez-faire* policies of the

Victorian era – after 1908. During these years he assumed the new guise of a Radical tribune, becoming one of the Liberals' foremost public speakers. Although he ceased to represent a Lancashire constituency in 1908, he was to remain a leading voice of Liberalism in this key electoral region. For much of this period his new parliamentary colleagues were unsure how to regard him, and he was never entirely at home in the Liberal ranks. His roots were shallow and he never had a personal following, though many Liberals enjoyed and applauded his verbal demolitions of the Conservatives. As always, Churchill was most comfortable in the company of the leading lights.

Churchill served his ministerial apprenticeship during the Campbell-Bannerman government. The post at the Colonial Office gave him unusual scope as the Secretary of State, Lord Elgin, a shy and mainly silent figure, was in the House of Lords and Churchill was solely responsible for representing the department in the House of Commons. Elgin determined the policy on major issues, but he listened to Churchill's views and allowed him scope in less crucial areas. The most important task was the settlement of South Africa after the bitterness of the Boer War. Churchill urged a generous solution to promote reconciliation, and influenced the substantial degree of self-government which was granted to the former Boer republics in 1906 and 1907. In the autumn of 1907 he embarked on a four-month tour of the east African colonies, which included some big-game hunting. Energetic and a fountain of ideas, Churchill was an obvious candidate for promotion. A mark of his rise was the conferment of a Privy Councillorship on 1 May 1907; he was now 'the Right Honourable', and entitled to precedence over ordinary MPs in debates in the House of Commons.

Despite their huge majority in the House of Commons, the government were soon in difficulties. By this period most of the aristocracy supported the Conservatives, and the opposition party used their resulting dominance in the House of Lords to wreck or reject the government's bills. (The House of Lords is the non-elected house of British legislature, which deliberates parliamentary issues and constitutes the most senior court in Britain. The House of Commons is the elected lower, but effectively the ruling, chamber of legislature.) The ministry seemed to be repeating the dismal experience of the last Liberal government of 1892–95, which had achieved nothing – disappointing its supporters and falling apart. 1908 was a black year, marked by the death of Campbell-Bannerman in April, but matters improved under his successor, H.H. Asquith. He reshuffled the cabinet, giving his former position as Chancellor of the Exchequer to Lloyd George and promoting Churchill to the resulting vacancy as President of the Board of Trade. At the age of only thirty-three Churchill had truly arrived in the front rank, for to be a British cabinet minister was to be one of the group of less than twenty men who determined the destiny of the most powerful nation and greatest empire the world had ever seen. One small hurdle caused a momentary stumble, for in this period the law still required a newly appointed minister to resign his seat and contest a by-election. Manchester North-West was a mainly

Churchill remained devoted to Clementine throughout his life, and there is no sign that he was ever interested in other women. Their mutual love was the bedrock of his life, and their family life gave him stability and security.

Conservative marginal that had been won on the free trade issue in 1906, but it now swung back. Although the Conservative press were exultant, Churchill's defeat on 23 April 1908 was little more than a nuisance; the Liberal whips swiftly found him a new and safer constituency in the Scottish industrial town of Dundee, and he was elected there on 9 May.

One other crucial event in Churchill's life occurred at this time: in March 1908 he met and fell in love with Clementine Hozier. Churchill was sociable in the company of men, but like many of his class was less certain with women; he was also, as he warned Clementine during their courtship, 'quite self-reliant and self-contained'. He had been attracted to two or three women during the previous decade, but his passions had been focused upon his political career and there had been room for little else in his life. Although that did not greatly change, his love for Clementine was deep and lasting. He courted her during the following months, and proposed during a walk in the gardens at Blenheim on 11 August. They were married at St Margaret's church in Westminster on 12 September 1908; Lord Hugh Cecil was best man and Lloyd George was one of the witnesses. Although her background was aristocratic – her grandfather was the Earl of Airlie – Clementine was not an obvious match for an ambitious young man. Her parents had separated when she was six; her mother had brought her up in modest circumstances, and she had no money of her own. At twenty-three she was ten years younger than her husband, an attractive and intelligent young woman of a serious disposition. Whilst she could be a charming hostess, many found her cool and reserved in manner.

Churchill remained devoted to Clementine throughout his life, and there is no sign that he was ever interested in other women. Their mutual love was the bedrock of his life, and their family life gave him stability and security. They had

very different temperaments, as Clementine was more pessimistic, worried about money and was uncomfortable with a lavish lifestyle. Her health was less robust, and Churchill tended to take for granted her role in managing the household and family affairs. She did not share all of his social life and disapproved of many of his political cronies, fearing the effects of their bad influence or reputations. Her judgement was often good, but her husband rarely took her advice and sometimes did not properly consult her – most seriously when he purchased the Chartwell estate in 1922 without telling her. They were both strong characters and there were occasional stormy scenes, but Clementine was always firmly behind her husband and there was no question that his needs came first. They kept different hours, as Churchill liked to work into the night and spend the morning in bed, working on his papers and dictating. Clementine rose and retired much earlier, and from an early stage they had separate bedrooms. It was

Clementine Churchill with their first child, Diana, at the seaside in 1910. *Curtis Brown/Broadwater Collection/ Churchill Archives Centre*

a successful marriage, but had its periods of tension and distance; however, it was customary in their era and class for husbands and wives to spend a good deal of time apart, and the Churchills were not particularly unusual in this. They sometimes needed a short rest from each other's company, but these separations served to reaffirm their mutual dependency. When apart they exchanged frequent and affectionate letters, using their pet names for each other – she was 'Kat' and he was 'Pug'. Their first child, Diana, was born in July 1909, and their second child and only son, named Randolph in memory of Winston's father, was born in May 1911. Three more girls followed: Sarah (born 1914), Marigold (born 1918, but died from an infection in 1921), and finally Mary (born 1922).

The other important connection which Churchill made in this period was a lasting friendship with David Lloyd George. As Chancellor of the Exchequer and the leading Radical in the cabinet, Lloyd George was the senior and weightier figure. His humble Welsh background was very different from Churchill's, but they were both something of outsiders to the English Liberal establishment. More importantly, their political temperaments had much in common. They favoured dynamic activity and unorthodox approaches, and both had a fascination for politics in general and their own position in particular. After Churchill's entry into the cabinet, they formed a vigorous and visionary combination which pushed forward a radical agenda on social reform. They also worked together on other issues, and their strenuous opposition to the increased naval estimates of 1908 caused a cabinet crisis. Lloyd George and Churchill had a practical approach to the role of the state and were willing to extend it to new areas where necessary. They were influenced by examples from the continent, and especially the social insurance system which Bismarck had constructed in Germany.

As well as promoting social reform in cabinet, Churchill contributed some measures of his own. As President of the Board of Trade, he was responsible for many industrial and employment issues. The exploitation of 'sweated labour' was addressed in the Trade Board Acts, which established machinery to regulate wage rates in a number of industries, and he also introduced two measures dealing with working conditions in the coal mines. He tackled unemployment directly by introducing Labour Exchanges, and played a part in the shaping of the social insurance scheme which became Lloyd George's National Insurance Act of 1911. Churchill always had sympathy for the conditions of the poor, and wanted to raise the minimum standards of living to decent and healthy levels. However, he did not aim to eliminate social differences. He accepted the existence of hierarchy (finding it natural to be dressed and attended by servants), and was appalled by the levelling agenda and 'class war' language of Socialism. The latter was gaining prominence during these years as the trade unions and the Labour Party expanded, and Churchill's vehement denunciations led to counter-charges that he was hostile to the working class.

He enjoyed the fray and always wanted to be at the centre of attention; convinced that he had the answers, he would sometimes push himself forwards recklessly.

In these Edwardian years Churchill established himself as a politician who commanded attention. His characteristic strengths became apparent, as did many of his weaknesses. Friends and foes recognised his audacity, brilliance, drive and energy. He had a tremendous capacity for work, dominating his material and never being daunted by a new challenge. He was a fount of original ideas, and his complete self-assurance led to bold and imaginative proposals. Many of these might be flawed or impracticable, but not all; he could try his colleagues' patience by ranging far beyond his own brief, but never exhausted it. He had the power of language to press his views home, both on paper and in speeches. The latter contained many striking phrases, although he could become washed away in his own rhetorical flood. He had unfailing courage and was always willing to stand in the forefront; this might be the position of greatest visibility and opportunity, but he never shirked the risks that came with it. He enjoyed the fray and always wanted to be at the centre of attention; convinced that he had the answers, he would sometimes push himself forwards recklessly. His force and flair made a positive contribution to every cabinet in which he sat, although he seemed to lack discrimination or a sense of proportion. Churchill often dismayed his colleagues, but he also fascinated and perplexed them. In the years before and after the First World War his capacity won the admiration of leading figures, but his self-interest and unpredictability meant that he had no personal following or strong party roots. This left him dependent upon the patronage of his seniors, and without a cushion if his fortunes should fall. His ambition was tolerated in part because it was so unconcealed; it was not his conduct that was distrusted, but his judgement. He could be infuriating and obstinate, bumptious and conceited, and was sometimes indiscreet and foolishly boastful. Even as his years advanced he continued to be thought of as a puckish, child-like personality – tempestuous but open, liable to go to extremes but without malice, holding no grudges against his opponents. His periods of depression were not exhibited to the outer world, to whom he appeared cheerful and bustling, more full of bounce than Tigger in the Winnie-the-Pooh stories.

For all of these reasons, Churchill became an increasingly prominent figure in the Liberal government. He made typically energetic and vivid contributions during the confrontation with the House of Lords over Lloyd George's 'People's Budget' of 1909. Churchill became chairman of the Liberal campaign organisation, the Budget League, and was one of the party's leading speakers in the general election of January 1910. The Liberals lost many of their landslide gains of 1906, but with Labour and Irish Nationalist support they remained in office. Although the Lords now passed the budget, the crisis was far from over. The Liberals were determined to prune the powers of the upper House, but the new King, George V, who suceeded to the throne in May 1910, required the confirmation of a further general election before he would promise to create as many new peers as necessary to ensure the passage of the government's reforms. This second election was held in December 1910, with results almost identical to those of January. The threat of a mass creation of Liberal peers led to the collapse of Conservative resistance in the summer of 1911, and the Liberals secured a landmark victory with the passage of the Parliament Act.

Churchill had been promoted after the January 1910 general election, and became Home Secretary on 14 February. This was one of the most senior and historic cabinet posts, and its many and varied responsibilities were to involve him in some controversial situations. On 3 January 1911 three policemen were killed by burglars armed with rifles who were trapped in a house in Stepney, in the slum districts of London's East End. Churchill authorised the use of troops and

Winston Churchill with his wife,
Clementine, during Territorial Army
manoeuvres at Aldershot in 1910.
PA Photos

visited what became known as the 'siege of Sidney Street' himself, viewing from nearby as the men in the house continued to shoot at the cordon of soldiers and police. Both criminals were killed during the siege, which ended with the house burning down. Churchill's only intervention was to instruct the fire brigade to stand back, but it was widely assumed that he had directed operations personally. He was criticised in the press for interference and overstepping his authority, and by Balfour in the House of Commons for exposing himself to needless danger. Once again, the impression was left of rashness, excessive self-confidence and love of the limelight.

Of more lasting significance for Churchill's political reputation were the industrial troubles which damaged his relations with the labour movement. He sent troops to south Wales after rioting during the miners' strike of November 1910, as a reserve if the police lost control. In fact they were not used, and Churchill was unfairly blamed for the casualties which occurred at Tonypandy. In the summer of 1911 he took a firm, even pugnacious, line during the dock and railway strikes. There was widespread rioting and looting, and he deployed troops on a much larger scale; on this occasion, two strikers were shot dead in a clash at Llanelli. The 'labour unrest' of these years was on a new and threatening scale, and the cabinet were behind Churchill's vigorous reaction to the disorder. However, his use of violent and alarmist language added to the crisis atmosphere, and his actions were seen as provocative by the labour movement. He was personally blamed for the bloodshed, which left a permanent legacy of hostility on the part of the trade unions and Labour Party. The labour movement had a long memory, and 'Tonypandy' was a cry raised by hecklers up to the Second World War. In other respects, Churchill was a reforming Home Secretary. He sought to reduce the number of people imprisoned by allowing more time for the payment of fines, and limited the use of solitary confinement.

Churchill's spell at the Home Office was unexpectedly cut short when he switched posts with Reginald McKenna and became First Lord of the Admiralty on 24 October 1911. He had been keen to have the Admiralty in January 1910, and the swap enabled Asquith to cool the temperature on the industrial front. The reason for moving McKenna sideways was the exposure of the navy's lack of war plans during the Agadir (or second Moroccan) crisis in the summer of 1911, which took Britain to the brink of war with Germany. Although otherwise an effective minister, McKenna had supported the admirals' view that a planning body was not needed; Churchill was instructed to remedy the deficiency, and rapidly instituted a naval war staff. Churchill always became absorbed in his departments but the Admiralty exerted a special fascination, appealing to his military interests and sense of history. The navy was the 'senior service' upon which British independence and trade depended, and maintaining Britain's position as the world's foremost naval power was a vital national interest. Churchill was exhilarated by his new responsibilities: he told Asquith's daughter it was 'the biggest thing that has ever come my way – the chance I should choose before all others. I shall pour into it everything I've got.' He did so in characteristic fashion: prying into every corner, mastering every detail, questioning traditional methods and upsetting the more conventional admirals along the way. They found him difficult and more intrusive than any previous minister, but many recognised his devotion to his post and his complete commitment to securing naval efficiency and supremacy.

Churchill had already been in contact with the most important naval figure of the day, Admiral 'Jacky' Fisher. The latter had transformed the navy after his appointment as First Sea Lord in 1904, but the controversies provoked by his combative methods had forced his retirement in 1910. Although Churchill decided against bringing Fisher back, he consulted him unofficially and fully supported his reforms. These had modernised the service, eliminated waste and improved the training of officers and the conditions of the lower ranks. Fisher's most striking innovation was intended to steal a march on rival powers: when HMS *Dreadnought* came into service in 1906 its speed and firepower completely outclassed anything afloat, and its name was adopted to describe the new type of battleship. Previously, Britain had avoided the risks of innovation and relied on its greater industrial capacity to outbuild its main rivals of France and Russia. However, the plans for a world-class navy unveiled in the German Navy Laws of 1898 and 1900 posed a more serious threat. The German economy was now overtaking Britain, and the establishment of such a powerful force in the North Sea had worrying implications for national security. During the nineteenth century, conflict had seemed most likely with Russia or France over imperial matters, but after 1900 this began to change as relations with Germany deteriorated. The Entente Cordiale of 1904 resolved the most important frictions with France and led to closer relations, and it was followed by a similar entente with Russia in 1907. The Edwardian era was marked by the development of Anglo-German antagonism, fostered by the increasing pace of the naval arms race and by unsuccessful German attempts to disrupt the ententes in the Moroccan crises of 1905–6 and 1911. By the time Churchill came to the Admiralty in the wake of the latter crisis, Germany was clearly identified as the power most hostile and dangerous to Britain.

This was recognised by changing the definition of naval security from the 'two-power standard' (dating from the rivalry with France and Russia) to a simple 60% margin over the next largest fleet, which now was Germany. Churchill's first priority was to maintain this lead against the threat of increasing German competition and domestic financial and political pressures. Fisher had already changed the distribution of naval forces in order to concentrate strength against Germany in home waters, and this trend continued. In 1912 the pressure of the naval race forced the recall of the last British capital ships stationed overseas. This led to an agreement under which the French moved their fleet to cover the Mediterranean and Britain took responsibility for the English Channel; whilst this did not categorically promise support for France in a war with Germany, it was hardly compatible with neutrality. Churchill pushed the development of more powerful battleships in the *Queen Elizabeth* class laid down in 1912; their speed and fifteen-inch gun armament was to be vastly superior to German ships at the Battle of Jutland in 1916, and they remained the core of the battlefleet during the Second World War. These were the first battleships to be fuelled by oil, and Churchill played a part in securing the source of supply through public control of the Anglo-Persian Oil Company (later British Petroleum). Churchill worked to prepare the fleet for the challenge of war in every possible way and, although the war exposed some deficiencies, he could justly claim that he had done everything in his power.

In the autumn of 1913 Churchill prepared a plan which would increase the

UNDER HIS MASTER'S EYE.

Scene—*Mediterranean, on board the Admiralty yacht "Enchantress."*

Mr. Winston Churchill. "ANY HOME NEWS?"

Mr. Asquith. "HOW CAN THERE BE WITH YOU HERE?"

battlefleet to seventy-nine ships by 1920, twenty more than previously estimated. He hoped that Germany would not be able to match this, and made a public offer to pause construction indefinitely if both sides agreed to do so. Churchill's proposed 'naval holiday' would have resulted in Britain retaining its existing margin of superiority without further expenditure, but it was taken by Germany as a sign that Britain was unable to sustain the pace; if anything, it made relations worse and encouraged further German building. The gesture was also designed to show public opinion at home, and especially in the Liberal Party, that the government was trying to reduce spending on armaments and improve the international atmosphere. The rejection of the 'naval holiday' led Churchill to bring forward considerably increased expenditure plans for 1914–15, leading to a cabinet confrontation with his former ally Lloyd George as the latter shaped his 1914 budget. To many Liberals, Churchill now seemed to be an uncritical expansionist, and his enthusiasm and interest in naval matters appeared too close to bellicosity. Radical concern in the cabinet and on the Liberal backbenches supported the Chancellor, whilst Churchill was adamant that the Admiralty proposals were the minimum required to preserve Britain's margin of safety. The cabinet debates dragged on for several weeks in January and February 1914, but Churchill doggedly defended his corner and in the end secured almost all that he had asked for. Lloyd George turned his attention to raising the revenue and finding economies elsewhere, and the reverse did not affect his friendship with Churchill.

The Admiralty years were a period of strenuous work, with frequent speaking in parliament and the country in addition to heavy departmental responsibilities. As a member of the cabinet, Churchill was involved in the major political issues of the day, including the curbing of the powers of the House of

Lords in 1911 and the bitter struggle over Home Rule for Ireland between 1912 and 1914. His main opportunity for relaxation was during the several weeks each year which he spent at sea visiting ships and bases, most frequently travelling on the Admiralty yacht, *Enchantress*. Churchill became an enthusiast for the new activity of flying and strenuously promoted this within the navy, building up the embryo Royal Naval Air Service. Never one to take a back seat, he determined to fly himself and took lessons during 1913 and 1914. The experience exhilarated him: after a flight in October 1913 he wrote to Clementine 'it has been as good as one of those old days in the S. African war, & I have lived entirely in the moment'. However, fatal accidents were frequent in these pioneering days of flimsy aircraft and no parachutes, and Clementine was understandably worried. After nearly 140 flights and close to qualifying as a pilot, he gave in to her pleas and stopped flying in June 1914.

When the events which led to the outbreak of the First World War unfolded in July 1914, the Liberal cabinet were pre-occupied with the crisis over Irish Home Rule. By fortunate chance a practice mobilisation of the whole fleet was in progress; on Sunday 26 July, only two days after the cabinet heard of the Austrian ultimatum to Serbia, Churchill countermanded the dispersal planned for the next day, and on 28 July he ordered the fleet to its war stations. When war was declared on 3 August the Royal Navy was in secure command of the English Channel and North Sea, and Churchill's swift action was widely praised for having avoided the danger of a surprise German strike. However, his next initiative was another matter entirely. In late September the key Belgian port of Antwerp was under heavy German attack, and its fall threatened to expose the Channel ports and the British Expeditionary Force's lines of communication. Churchill not only threw in the lightly equipped Royal Naval Division to shore up the Belgian defence but also arrived in person, driving around the city in an open Rolls Royce. Typically, he became caught up in the drama of the moment, and on 5 October caused amazement with a telegram to Asquith offering to resign from the cabinet in order to command the defence of Antwerp. This seemed wildly impetuous and to show a complete loss of proportion; the Antwerp affair dented Churchill's credibility and made him seem a strategic danger, especially as the city soon fell and many of the troops that he had sent were captured.

The naval war did not produce the decisive battle that the public had anticipated, and turned into a long waiting game of blockade and patrol. The handful of German cruisers based in their colonial possessions in Africa and the Far East were rapidly eliminated, although not without some difficult moments. The popular anti-German hysteria forced Prince Louis of Battenberg to resign as First Sea Lord, and Churchill decided to recall Fisher. They worked well together at first, but the mixture of two such egotistical and domineering personalities in a situation where their spheres of responsibility overlapped was likely to have explosive consequences. The rift came over Churchill's diversion of resources to the Mediterranean for an attempt to knock Turkey out of the war by an assault on its capital. A naval attack through the Dardanelles was attempted in March 1915 but failed, alerting the Turks to the danger. When several weeks later 30,000 troops were landed on the Gallipoli peninsula they met strong resistance and incurred heavy casualties. Despite reinforcements and a further landing in August, the Gallipoli campaign turned into a costly and humiliating disaster. The casualty lists grew longer without any gains, and finally in January 1916 the exhausted British forces had to be evacuated. The campaign was one of the worst reverses of the war, and Churchill incurred most of the blame. This was not entirely fair,

No other operation in this part of the
world cd ever cloak the defeat of
abandoning the effort against the
Dardanelles. I think there is nothing
for it but to go through with the
business, & I do not at all regret
that this shd be so. No one can
count with certainty upon the
issue of a battle. But here we
have the chances in our favour, &
play for vital gains with non-
vital stakes.

Yours & mine,

Winston S. Churchill

as some of the blunders and missed opportunities were due to failures of the commanders on the spot. However, Churchill had been the strongest advocate of the operation and carried other ministers with him in his enthusiasm, and now became the convenient scapegoat. With hindsight, the affair seemed to demonstrate many of his defects: although over-ambitious and poorly conceived, Churchill had pursued his plan with reckless fervour, dismissing any contrary advice. The later public inquiry damaged his reputation, and the fiasco of Gallipoli was to count against him for the rest of his career.

The political consequences were swift and severe, and led to the lowest point of Churchill's career. He had ignored or over-ridden Fisher's objections, and on 15 May 1915 the First Sea Lord resigned. This would have been a severe crisis for the government in any event, but it also coincided with the exposure of failures in the supply of shells to the Western Front. The result was the end of Britain's last Liberal government, as Asquith negotiated its replacement by an all-party Coalition. The Conservatives had to be given at least one major ministry, and they made Churchill's removal from the Admiralty an essential condition for joining the government. This was not just the legacy of pre-war hostility, for they had no confidence in Churchill as a wartime minister and Fisher's resignation confirmed their view that he was a national danger in his present post. During the following days Churchill lobbied with increasing desperation to stay at the Admiralty, but he was politically isolated and had to accept the inevitable. On 21 May he wrote to Asquith accepting 'any office – the lowest if you like – that you care to offer me'. Churchill's stock had fallen so far that he was given the least of cabinet posts, as Chancellor of the Duchy of Lancaster. This had no significant responsibilities and Churchill was almost completely sidelined; his only consolation was continued membership of the

cabinet and the crucial Dardanelles Committee. He languished in frustration, and six months later was excluded when the Dardanelles Committee was replaced by an inner cabinet 'War Committee'. On 11 November 1915 – after almost exactly a decade in office – he resigned from the government. With nothing worthwhile to do at Westminster, he offered his services to the army and a few weeks later was in the trenches of the Western Front. To many – including for a time Churchill himself – it seemed that his career was over, ending like his father with a meteoric downfall caused mainly by the flaws in his own character.

3

Navigating the shoals 1915–1929

By 1915, at the age of forty, Churchill had already left in his wake more disturbance and controversy than most politicians create in a lifetime. Whether fairly or not, 'Tonypandy' and 'Gallipoli' were to be cries raised against him for the next quarter of a century, and the doubts and hostility he had engendered would be difficult to overcome. This was the darkest hour of his career, and for a while after May 1915 he was overwhelmed by frustration and despair. 'When he left the Admiralty he thought he was finished', Clementine later recalled; she feared 'he would die of grief', and was herself in constant tears.

Churchill always needed to occupy himself, for inactivity led to brooding and the bouts of depression which he called his 'Black Dog'. This was the stimulus behind his love of travel and new experiences, and the energy which he devoted to every part of his life, whether work or leisure. At this bleak point Churchill was helped by the discovery of painting, which he tried at the suggestion of his sister-in-law one day in the summer of 1915. It absorbed him – painting was the only activity that he conducted in silence – and had great therapeutic value. Churchill considered it 'complete as a distraction'; whilst working on a picture his cares would fall away and 'time stands respectfully aside'. He never needed this more than now, and painting became the favourite pastime of the rest of his life. His subjects were landscapes, which he painted out-of-doors. The style was conventional but not always simple realism; as in politics, he brought a sense of drama to his compositions. His brushwork was bold and decisive, with 'fierce strokes and slashes'. Churchill's work has received some favourable comment but was essentially of good amateur quality, and it is doubtful if there would still be interest if the pictures were by another hand. Painting was never intended to earn money, unlike his other craft of writing. The latter was a much more public activity, often with a team of research

Previous page: Churchill in the uniform
of a Privy Councillor, 1915.
Henry Guttmann/Getty Images

assistants and typists, and whilst it could engage his energy it could never be purely a source of relaxation.

During the fretful summer and autumn of 1915 Churchill's thoughts had turned to active military service, and he put this plan into immediate effect after his resignation in November. He crossed to France on 18 November, and within a few days got some experience in the trenches. His unrealistic aspirations for a substantial command were turned down, and he was commissioned as a Lieutenant-Colonel and offered a battalion. From 5 January to 3 May 1916 he commanded the 6th battalion of the Royal Scots Fusiliers with all his usual zest and vigour. The battalion was resting and training, and returned to the front line at Ploegsteert in Flanders at the end of January. Churchill was never required to lead his men 'over the top', but neither was this a backwater; it was an average section of the line in winter, with all its attendant miseries and intermittent dangers. Churchill was always near the front and made thirty-six reconnaissance trips into the 'no man's land' between the opposing armies; he was twice nearly killed, but emerged unscathed. However, he could not see this as a proper use of his talents, and he hankered to return to a position of influence. During a short leave in March 1916 he spoke in the House of Commons on the naval war, but ruined the effect with the bizarre suggestion that Fisher be reappointed. His intervention was a humiliating failure, reminding everyone of his capacity for misjudgement. Even so, when his command lapsed due to his battalion being merged with another, he decided to return to civilian life.

The road back to office was still barred, and during the second half of 1916 Churchill occupied himself with journalism and preparing his evidence for the inquiry into the Dardanelles and Gallipoli campaign. Rehabilitation was essential if his career was to recover; although the report in March 1917 contained some

criticism, the blame was spread more widely and he was no longer exposed to
sole attack. By this time Asquith was no longer Prime Minister: in December
1916 he was ousted by Lloyd George, who constructed a closer Coalition
between part of the Liberal Party and the Conservatives. The latter made
exclusion of Churchill a condition of joining, and he was bitterly disappointed
to be left out. However, in the spring of 1917 Churchill began to emerge
from the cloud of Gallipoli, and his speeches in the House of Commons were
becoming more effective. Lloyd George was aware of his capacity and used a
reshuffle of posts to make him Minister of Munitions on 17 July 1917. He was
outside the War Cabinet and had no influence over strategy, but even so the bitter
Conservative protests shook the Coalition. The hostility of Conservative MPs and

the press underlined the extent to which Churchill's return was dependent upon Lloyd George's support, and their relationship continued to be central to his career for a further decade.

During the next five years Churchill's successful conduct of three departments was to restore him to the front rank, although Gallipoli remained a shadow on his reputation up to 1940. The Ministry of Munitions was a wartime innovation resulting from the need for huge quantities of weapons and ammunition for the newly raised mass army, especially the vast number of shells used in the artillery barrages of the Western Front. Problems of supply led to the Ministry being created under Lloyd George in May 1915, and the latter's vigour and success in the post played a key part in his rise to the Premiership in 1916. Lloyd George had achieved much in a whirlwind of activity, but his successors had become entangled in detail and bottlenecks were occurring. Churchill swiftly introduced a supervisory board to shoulder much of the detail and improved efficiency by reducing the fifty departments to ten. The most important concern was that industrial disputes would disrupt production. The cost of living was rising and the expansion of factories had resulted in the 'dilution' of skilled labour by untrained workers, which eroded wage differentials. Churchill took a generous line and proposed a significant wage increase for the vital skilled men, and serious strikes were avoided. He spent a considerable amount of time visiting the front in France, ostensibly to see what was needed. He warned of a German offensive in the spring, and when this came in March 1918 reacted quickly to speed the necessary supplies. His other important contribution was the development of a new weapon – the 'tank'. In January 1915 Churchill had suggested that a caterpillar-tracked and armoured 'land ship' would be able to cross the mud, barbed wire and machine-gun fire of the trenches. Before leaving the Admiralty

During the next five years Churchill's successful conduct of three departments was to restore him to the front rank, although Gallipoli remained a shadow on his reputation up to 1940.

he set up a Landships Committee, which led to the development of the first tanks. As Minister of Munitions he now gave the new weapon a further boost, giving it priority in production and urging its use on a large scale. The army command was slow to see the potential, but tank attacks played an important part in the advances of autumn 1918, which led to the sudden German collapse and the Armistice in November.

Churchill supported Lloyd George's decision to continue the Coalition into peacetime; his relations with the Conservative leaders had improved since 1917, and this was his only route to office. The strains of the war had severely weakened the Liberal Party, and it was bitterly divided by Lloyd George's ousting of Asquith in 1916. In the general election of December 1918, the Liberal MPs who did not support Lloyd George bore the brunt of public blame for the problems of the early stages of the war: Asquith lost his own seat, and only 28 of his followers were elected. Although they had only 57 MPs, the Labour Party emerged as the main opposition to the Coalition, which won 473 seats (of which 382 were Conservatives). Churchill's position still largely depended upon the Prime Minister, but he was the most prominent figure from the pre-war cabinet to support Lloyd George and this helped to preserve the Liberal credentials of the Coalition. After the election the government was reshaped, and Churchill returned to the cabinet as Secretary of State for War and Air on 10 January 1919. This might seem an odd choice in view of his Admiralty record, but with the end of the war it was a less important and visible position – the main controversies would now be on domestic issues. Churchill's first concern was demobilising the army, as unrest and even mutinies were flaring up due to delays and injustices. He resolved this with a simple and fairer scheme based on the principle of 'first in, first out', and during the next few months 2.5 million personnel were returned to civilian status. Under the pressure to economise, during 1919 Churchill reduced the army from 3 million to a force of 370,000. However, it still retained considerable responsibilities throughout the world, and these had been expanded by the acquisition of large areas in the Middle East after the defeat of the Ottoman Empire. The sudden collapse of the enemy powers in late 1918 left Britain with no immediate threats, and in August 1919 Churchill secured cabinet endorsement of the 'ten year rule'. This laid down that defence spending could be planned on the assumption that Britain would not be involved in a major war during the next decade, and was later blamed for Britain's weak position in the 1930s.

Churchill's major theme in these post-war years was the danger of 'Bolshevism'. This was not just the hostile new regime in Russia, for the chaos after the collapse of the enemy powers saw revolutionary risings spread across central Europe. At home the strains of demobilisation and the return to a peacetime economy led to serious industrial unrest, and 1919–21 was the most unstable and alarming period of the whole inter-war era. Churchill was horrified by Communism, which he regarded as an evil and tyrannical regime, malevolently working to destroy liberty and the constitution and undermine the empire. He was not alone in his reaction, but due to his cabinet position and oratorical powers he was particularly visible. In speech after speech Churchill denounced the 'Red menace' in lurid language, and there was a feeling that he was losing his balance and becoming obsessed. This was particularly the case with his advocacy of intervening in the Russian civil war, which fell on deaf ears both at the Paris Peace Conference in February 1919 and in the cabinet at home. The country was war weary and there was no desire for further entanglements, and in October 1919 the last British forces were withdrawn from the ports in the Arctic

north, where they had been guarding the military supplies delivered during the war. With Lloyd George often absent at the peace conference during 1919, Churchill had been able to secure reluctant agreement from the cabinet for assisting the 'White' anti-Soviet forces in the civil war with loans and munitions. However, the expenditure of £100 million by the end of 1919 did not prevent their defeat, and Lloyd George finally insisted that all British involvement must end. The affair seemed to be another Churchill failure, in which his fervour had again blinded him to the realities of the situation. It had further provoked the Soviet regime, which had to be dealt with as the effective government, and inflamed the attitudes of the labour movement at home. However, for the first time since the decision to declare war in 1914, Churchill was taking the same line as the Conservative right, and 'anti-Socialism' was the common ground which began to draw him back to his former party. At the same time, his persistent advocacy of intervention strained his relations with Lloyd George, and eroded his remaining credibility as a Liberal.

On 15 February 1921 Churchill moved posts again, this time to become Secretary of State for the Colonies, the department at which he had begun as junior minister in 1905. The Colonial Office was responsible for the direct administration of the British colonial empire and for relations with the largely self-governing Dominions of Canada, South Africa, Australia and New Zealand.

The only areas for which Churchill was not responsible were India, which had its own ministry in London and a Viceroy and government in Delhi, and Egypt, which came under the Foreign Office. Churchill's remit was therefore vast and varied, but the most pressing issues concerned the recently acquired territories in the Middle East. Large parts of the former Ottoman Empire had been given to Britain in the peace settlement, in the form of 'mandates' from the new League of Nations, and the arrangements for these needed to be determined. Already familiar with the problems of the region from his previous post at the War Office, Churchill moved quickly and convened a special conference of British officials at Cairo in March 1921. This established Arab kingdoms in Jordan and Iraq as the recognised local government, retaining overall British influence without the costs and difficulties of direct control. Another aspect of the drive for economy was Churchill's reliance upon air power as a cheap method of keeping the peace in the remoter regions of the empire, and this was particularly effective in desert regions such as Iraq. Churchill established a special Middle East Department within the Colonial Office, and took advice from experts including the wartime hero of Arab liberation, T.E. Lawrence. He also confirmed the Balfour Declaration of 1917 which had promised the Jews a 'national home' in Palestine, now also a British mandate. Churchill was a favourable to Zionism throughout his life, and believed that Jewish immigration would improve the conditions for all in these poor and undeveloped lands. Although generally optimistic he recognised that tensions could increase, and barred Jewish settlement beyond the river Jordan.

A major problem since 1919 had been the 'troubles' in Ireland, and whilst at the War Office Churchill had been involved in the attempt to defeat the Sinn Fein rebellion by repression. During 1920 he was in favour of a firm policy and

Churchill's greatest relaxation was painting landscapes; this was part of the garden at Trent Park, New Barnet, Hertfordshire, the home of his friend, the Conservative MP Sir Philip Sassoon; it is now part of Middlesex University. The painting hangs at Chartwell Manor in Kent.
Curtis Brown © Churchill Heritage/ Bridgeman Art Library

supporting the police with extra forces, but the latter's indiscipline and use of reprisals only aroused further opposition. When the introduction of martial law in the disturbed areas failed to suppress the guerrilla activity, Churchill accepted that a political solution was the only way forward given the rising level of domestic and international criticism. Although remaining firm in public, in the cabinet from early 1921 he was urging a truce and negotiations. When these came about he was a leading figure in the group of senior ministers who met with the Sinn Fein delegates at Downing Street from October 1921. When agreement was achieved in early December, Churchill was given the task of steering the treaty through the House of Commons. This was a delicate matter, especially as the Conservative backbenchers upon whom the Coalition government depended were restive over the 'U-turn' and concessions to rebels. Churchill took great care and delivered one of his finest and most effective speeches when introducing the measure on 16 December, and the tact and skill with which he secured its acceptance raised his prestige.

By 1922 Churchill had become one of the most powerful figures in the Coalition cabinet, and together with his close friend F.E. Smith (now the Earl of Birkenhead) was one of the inner circle who set its tone. Another sign of his growing strength was that Lloyd George began to be wary and suspicious of his ambitions, and their relationship had difficult periods in 1921 and 1922. The Prime Minister's own position was slipping as the government ran into problems on almost every front, and Churchill's independence and increasing closeness to the leading Conservatives was a potential danger. However, the crisis which ended the Coalition in October 1922 came from another direction, and found all of the leading figures in the cabinet united. Churchill had opposed Lloyd George's support for Greek ambitions in Asia Minor, but when this collapsed and the victorious Turkish nationalist forces advanced towards the Straits he became concerned that British interests and the gains of the war were being threatened. He swung round to a publicly belligerent attitude, drafting an official telegram to the governments of the Dominions of Canada, South Africa, Australia and New Zealand which caused alarm and offence and left Britain exposed to a possible war without their support. The restraint of the British commander on the spot secured a peaceful outcome when British and Turkish troops confronted each other at Chanak on the shores of the Straits, but the crisis had now become a political one. It had raised the question of the future of the Coalition, as Lloyd George, Churchill and the leading Conservatives in the cabinet sought to rush a general election and exploit the crisis atmosphere. They were unexpectedly thwarted by a revolt from below in the Conservative Party, and the government was brought down when Conservative MPs at the Carlton Club meeting of 19 October 1922 voted overwhelmingly against continuing the Coalition. Lloyd George immediately resigned as Prime Minister; although he remained a powerful force, he was never to hold office again.

Bonar Law had emerged from retirement to lead the rebels, and accepted office as Prime Minister. He formed a government from the Conservative anti-Coalitionists, and at once dissolved parliament. The general election of November 1922 led to the second major interruption in Churchill's career. He not only had lost office with the fall of the Lloyd George Coalition, but also was to be out of the House of Commons for nearly two years. Liberal Coalitionism was discredited by 1922: there had been too many failures, scandals, changes of direction and illiberal policies. The Lloyd George government had been unpopular and unemployment was rising, and like many other industrial working-class constituencies, Dundee swung to Labour. Churchill had an even heavier handicap, for on the day before the Coalition fell he had been operated upon for acute appendicitis, and he was still convalescing when the election began. Clementine took his place and fought valiantly, but the public mood was hostile. Still in pain, Churchill travelled north and struggled through the last four days of the campaign, carried onto the platform in an invalid chair. Defeat had probably been inevitable, and when the votes were counted he was out by a margin of almost 10,000.

After this setback, the Churchills rented a house in Cannes on the French Riviera for six months, where he recuperated and worked on *The World Crisis*. This was a sweeping and powerful history of the war which included an element of personal memoir and justification, and it appeared in five volumes between 1923 and 1931. He was paid a £40,000 advance for the work; this was a great deal of money – in comparison, an MP's annual salary was only £400 at this time. Together with a recent legacy, this stabilised the Churchill finances and compensated for the loss of his ministerial salary. It also covered the purchase of Chartwell, an Elizabethan manor house with an estate of eighty acres, set in a picturesque position in the heart of the Kentish countryside, near Westerham. It had captured Churchill's heart and he acquired it for £5,000 in September 1922, ignoring Clementine's opposition. For all its potential and charm, the property was badly run down and the long restoration was to cost nearly £18,000. Clementine never loved Chartwell as her husband did, but it became

his haven and delight. He closely supervised the redesign of the house, lake and grounds, finding a new hobby in brick-laying (and even becoming a member of the bricklayers' trade union).

British politics were in a confused state in 1923, with the Liberal Party fractured and the ousted Conservative leaders sulking in their tents as Bonar Law's inexperienced cabinet drifted towards the rocks. Churchill was not alone in the wilderness, but his position was the most indefinite. The coalition arrangement had suited him, and like its other leaders he had hopes that it might be revived. As these dwindled, his lack of a party base became a more serious drawback. There was to be one last outing as a Liberal. Bonar Law's health

collapsed in May 1923; his unexpected successor, Stanley Baldwin, caused even
more surprise and consternation by calling a general election in December 1923
to seek a mandate for tariff reform. Churchill was still a defender of free trade,
and in this sudden revival of the old controversy he was adopted as Liberal
candidate for Leicester West, but lost to Labour. Tariff reform was again
electorally unpopular, and the election reduced the Conservatives to 258 MPs,
against 191 for Labour and 158 for the Liberals (who had temporarily reunited
in defence of free trade). The free trade parties combined to defeat Baldwin when
the new parliament assembled in January 1924, and the Labour Party took office
for the first time, with the tacit support of the Liberals. This widened the gap
between both wings of the Liberal Party and the Conservatives, and Churchill
was left without a congenial home. His move away from the Liberals was partly
because they were in disarray and unlikely to hold power in the near future, but
mainly due to the primacy he put upon opposition to Socialism. This carried
him naturally back to the Conservatives, but changing party a second time would
require some finesse: as Churchill himself remarked, anyone could 'rat' once,
but it took 'a certain amount of ingenuity to re-rat'.

In the event, the return to the Conservative Party was much less
controversial than the departure had been. It was just one more aspect of the
turmoil and changes of post-war politics, and seemed logical in view of his
onslaughts on the 'Red menace' since 1919. Because of this, there were
comparatively few charges of opportunism, although many Conservatives had
reservations. These were not the legacy of 1904 or of his Liberal career; they had
a much more recent cause – his prominence amongst the Coalitionists. Under
its new leadership, the Conservative Party had vehemently rejected anti-Socialist
deals with Liberals in favour of a simple two-party system, in which the clear

alternatives were Conservative or Labour and the Liberals had no place. However, fears of plots to revive the Coalition were a constant theme in Conservative politics from 1922 to 1935. The whiff of potential intrigue hung around the former Coalitionists, but here Churchill was in the same boat as Austen Chamberlain, Birkenhead, Balfour and Horne – all lifelong Conservatives. Crucially, Baldwin was keen to ease Churchill's return to the Conservative Party as part of recapturing the centre ground lost in the 1923 election, and the dropping of the rejected tariff programme in February 1924 helped to clear the way.

Although he could not immediately adopt the party label, Churchill began to make speeches from Conservative platforms and Central Office was looking for a suitable seat. However, Churchill's inability to wait caused problems once again. He could not resist the vacancy at the Abbey division of Westminster, one of the safest Conservative seats in the country, and rushed into the fray as an 'Independent Anti-Socialist'. His action divided Conservatives nationally and locally, and he attracted considerable support even though an official Conservative candidate was also nominated. The lively contest caught public attention, but his loss to the official Conservative by only 43 votes was perhaps the best outcome – the campaign showed his force, without doing actual damage. On 23 September 1924 he was adopted as candidate by the Conservative association in Epping, and in the Conservative landslide victory of the following month he was elected with a majority of 9,763 votes. He fought the election as a 'Constitutional and Anti-Socialist', and only officially rejoined the Conservative Party a few weeks later. He was to remain the MP for this constituency for the rest of his career, although in 1945 the boundaries were revised and its name was changed to Woodford. This area to the north of London was becoming less rural as the middle-class suburbs

spread outwards, but it was solid Conservative territory and at last Churchill
had a secure base.

In one bound Churchill found himself back in the front rank. When
Baldwin formed his government in early November 1924 he amazed many
by appointing Churchill as Chancellor of the Exchequer – this was far above
Churchill's hopes, and when the offer was made at first he thought it was the
minor post of Chancellor of the Duchy of Lancaster. This was indeed the return
of the prodigal son, even if not to universal rejoicing. In fact, once Baldwin had
decided to bring Churchill into the cabinet, the choice of the Treasury was not
so surprising. The previous Conservative occupant, Neville Chamberlain,
preferred instead to take the Ministry of Health, where he planned to bring in
a major reform programme. The Treasury was in less direct contact with the
labour movement than other departments, an important consideration as Baldwin
wanted to encourage conciliation and moderation in industry. It had plenty to
occupy Churchill, and this elevation commanded his loyalty and separated him
from Lloyd George. The appointment as Chancellor did not go to Churchill's
head; he had plenty of ideas, but put the greatest emphasis upon loyalty to
Baldwin and being a reliable member of the cabinet team. He got on well with
the Prime Minister, and they had an easy working relationship with frequent
informal chats, visiting through the connecting door between 10 Downing Street
and number 11, the Chancellor's official residence.

The period as Chancellor from 1924 to 1929 was one of the happiest and
most settled phases of Churchill's career. He was almost at the top, and even more
importantly had equalled his father's highest achievement – when offered the
post, he referred emotionally to the fact that he still had his father's robes of
office. He was at his best in the House of Commons, effective in debate and

adding power to the government front bench. His speeches were lively and entertaining, the best political show in town – although this had the curious effect that they did not leave a lasting impression. His dexterity and ingenuity as Chancellor was admired, although he was not entirely convincing as an economic expert. Churchill still looked for the grand gesture and novel idea, and tended to sweep aside problems of detail. However, he formed a powerful working partnership with Neville Chamberlain, whose rigorous and practical approach provided the necessary balance. Although there were some frictions, the two were responsible for the government's most ambitious measures.

Churchill was happy with the moderate tone of the government and his first budget, delivered on 28 April 1925, introduced a significant reform by extending the state pensions scheme to cover widows and orphans. He also announced the return to the pre-war system of the gold standard, at the pre-war exchange rate of $4.86 to the pound. This had already been planned and almost all bankers and economists were in favour, but Churchill was doubtful and embarked on a thorough investigation. He consulted widely inside and outside the Treasury, including the leading critic, the radical economist John Maynard Keynes. However, restoring the gold standard was strongly urged by the most senior Treasury officials and the influential Governor of the Bank of England, Montagu Norman, and the weight of opinion in favour was overwhelming. It had become a symbol of the return to normality, and it was believed that returning to gold would stabilise the exchanges, leading to a revival of trade and the reduction of unemployment. Churchill had no real alternative, and suppressed his misgivings and accepted the prevailing view. Any other course would have been controversial and strongly criticised in financial circles, and he was keen to demonstrate that he was a sound and orthodox Chancellor. However, returning at the old parity over-valued the pound, making exports more difficult and adding to Britain's economic problems. Unemployment did not decrease and trade remained stagnant. Churchill rarely admitted to error, but became convinced that he had been mistaken. In fact, the return to gold contributed to the severe depression which followed the Wall Street Crash in 1929, and the British government was forced to abandon the gold standard at the height of the economic crisis in September 1931.

The other theme of his tenure at the Treasury also came to be questioned with the wisdom of hindsight. The pressing demand for reductions in government spending was another aspect of the desire to recover pre-war 'normality', and Churchill was assiduous in his search for economies. He became a cost-cutting Chancellor, and his range of ministerial experience and ability to put his case made him a formidable opponent. Social expenditure could not be slashed, but the absence of serious foreign rivals in the 1920s made the armed services a prime target. Churchill clashed with the Admiralty over its construction programme, and there was a major dispute in 1925. He saw no need to build up naval strength and dismissed fears of a future danger from Japan, slowing the work on the Singapore naval base almost to standstill. In 1942 these were decisions which were to return and haunt him.

The most serious challenge which the government faced was the General Strike of 4–12 May 1926, a national stoppage in support of the coal miners. Churchill was not one of the group of ministers involved in the negotiations with the Trade Union Congress leaders before the strike, as it was feared that he would be too aggressive and provocative. Once the General Strike began, his view was the same as Baldwin's: that this was a challenge to the constitution which must be defeated. However, his pugnacious instincts came to the fore, and

FIRST DAY OF GREAT STRIKE

Not So Complete as Hoped by its Promoters

PREMIER'S AUDIENCE OF THE KING

Miners and the General Council Meet at House of Commons

The great strike began yesterday. There are already signs, however, that it is by no means so complete as its promoters hoped. There were far more trains running than was the case on the first day of the railway strike in 1919.

The King received the Prime Minister in audience at Buckingham Palace yesterday morning.

Reports from all parts of the country indicate that satisfactory arrangements have been set up for recruiting. Volunteers came forward in large numbers in London and all the important provincial centres.

STRIKE LEADERS' MEETINGS.

The strike leaders have made no move, and the next step is with them.

The Executive of the Miners' Federation held a meeting yesterday morning at their headquarters. There was practically no business, and the officials then went to Eccleston-square, where the General Council of the Trades Union Congress were holding a meeting.

From Eccleston-square the whole Council, together with Mr. Herbert Smith, Mr. Cook, and Mr. Richardson (the miners' officials), went to the House of Commons. Mr. Ramsay MacDonald and Mr. Arthur Henderson had gone there and all were carried.

During the afternoon and late hours Executive was sent for to the House of Commons to hold a conference with the General Council of the Trades Union Congress, and the leaders of the Trade Union Congress special committee afterwards returned to Eccleston-square for a further meeting.

SPIRIT OF PUBLIC SERVICE.

Reports reaching the Government yesterday morning from the various areas into which the country is divided show that labour generally is quiet.

Recruiting stations have been opened in most parts of the country, and large numbers of volunteers have already enrolled.

RECRUITING STATIONS.

The following recruiting stations for volunteers in the London area are open:

Hornsey Area: Finsbury Crouch District Council Offices; Muswell Hill, Hornsey U.D.C., and narrow U.D.C.

Leyton District Area: Woodford U.D.C. Offices; Waltham Cross U.D.C.; Ilford U.D.C.; and Leyton U.D.C.

Hammersmith Area: Marylebone Town Hall; Ealing U.D.C.; Kensington Town Hall; Hammersmith and Westminster City Hall.

Bethnal Green Area: The Guildhall; Hackney Public Library; Islington Old Town Hall; and Stoke Newington Public Library.

Wandsworth Area: Lambeth Town Hall; Wandsworth Town Hall; Rich-

A MUSHROOM TOWN

The services of some of these volunteers were maintained in Hyde Park which, closed to the general public, controls the milk supply of London. At night the familiar green stretches had changed into a mushroom town of canvas activity. Thus and tents had sprung up, each with an appropriate notice as to the occupation housed therein, and each in charge of competent staffs, who took to their unaccustomed offices with marvellous rapidity. One of the officials in charge of the milk post stated that the organisation was almost perfect. "When you consider the circumstances," he said, "something in the nature of a miracle has been achieved."

The commissariat arrangements for the vast number of men and women who pass through the park during the day last night are in full swing. In a large marquee, never ceased supplying hot drinks and food at the minimum price.

The milk lorries themselves form one continuous line from end to end and close to side of the park. They bring the milk in from the farms, report to the transport officials, and receive instructions as to its distribution in London. Yesterday everybody seemed cheerful and hopeful, but quite prepared, in the worst case of the works, to carry on their new activities industriously.

LONDONERS' TREK TO WORK

On foot, squeezed into cars, standing in vans, riding pillion, jog-trot on cycles, swarming Cityward; by every road last night, London came yesterday morning doggedly and cheerfully to work.

Whoever has struggled along the chokest highway to London town on Derby Day may form a mental picture of the last day's worst pilgrimage to the East of Temple Bar. The congestion was as bad, and the temper of the people was as good.

No newspaper came to many houses to tell whether the conflict had at the eleventh hour been averted, but to read the news one had only to look out of the window. The streets with their press of private vehicles, with their streams of walkers settled to a long and steady stride, and, walk never a sign of bus or omnibus or clanging tram, told emphatically as print that the great general

FOOD SUPPLIES

No Hoarding: A Fair Share for Everybody

The Government is endeavouring to see that every person has a fair share of food and it is therefore of the greatest importance that every member of the public should assist in maintaining a fair distribution of supplies. They should do this by refraining from buying more than their usual quantities of foodstuffs.

Retailers should co-operate in securing a fair distribution of their stocks.

Bakers generally are holding satisfactory stocks of flour and coal.

The Executive Committee, appointed by the London Division Exchange, unanimously agreed that all market prices established on Friday last for all kinds of butter, cheese, bacon, ham, and lard shall remain the maximum prices until further notice.

In some parts of the provinces there seems to be an inclination to put up prices, partly caused by a certain amount of panic buying, which, however, is being checked by the traders and Co-operative Societies themselves.

Some fish has been sent to London from Lowestoft by sea.

Milk services are being well maintained.

MILK DISTRIBUTION

Control of Supplies in the Metropolis

The Deputy Chief Civil Commissioner's Office yesterday issued the following from the Board of Trade:

The Milk Distribution (Emergency) Order, 1926, dated 3rd May, 1926, made by the Board of Trade under the powers conferred upon them by Regulation 4 of the Emergency Regulations, 1926.

The above is a Trade, in exercise of the powers conferred upon them by Regulation 4 of the Emergency Regulations, 1926, and by all other powers them thereunto enabling, hereby make the following Order:—

(1) Every person owning or having power to act or dispose of any milk within the Metropolitan Police Area of London shall do any work required by the London Area Milk Committee's posts under mark at that Committee's disposal.

(2) Infringements of this Order are summary offences under the Emergency Regulations, 1926.

(3) This Order may be cited as the Milk Distribution (Emergency) Order, 1926.

H. A. PAYNE,
A Secretary to the Board of Trade.

LAW COURTS AT WORK

Judge on the Duty of the Public

All the Judges in the Probate, Divorce, and Admiralty Divisions took their seats at the appointed time yesterday morning. Several being a Bench Judges were able to proceed with the trial of actions, but others had to delay proceedings because of late arrivals. Mr. Justice Horridge, in releasing a waiting jury, asked them to be in attendance at a quarter-past ten on Wednesday morning. "It is a public duty," he said, "and we must do the best we can."

When Mr. Justice Lawrence arrived late he said he had been two hours and a half coming. Mr. Justice Hill stated that it had taken him two hours to travel from Wimbledon.

Mr. Justice Astbury said he did not propose to take any action in which the witnesses lived at any material distance. It would be a gross injustice to do so.

The spacious yard on the western side

HOLD-UP OF THE NATION

Government and the Challenge

NO FLINCHING

The Constitution or a Soviet

When King and People understand each other past a doubt,
It takes a foe and more than a foe to knock that country out.
                   Kipling.

"Be strong and quit yourselves like men."

The general strike is in operation, expressing in no uncertain terms a direct challenge to ordered government. It would be futile to attempt to minimise the seriousness of such a challenge, constituting as it does an effort to force upon some 42,000,000 British citizens the will of less than 4,000,000 others engaged in the vital services of the country.

The strike is intended as a direct hold-up of the nation to ransom. It is for the nation to stand firm in its determination not to flinch. "This moment," as the Prime Minister pointed out in the House of Commons, "has been called to choose whether we shall submit to the reign of force or not what would now exists ...

If a general strike were to be allowed to succeed it would be the end of democratic freedom. ...

THE CHOICE

"The country and Parliament, which represents the nation, is confronted

COMMUN... ARR

Mr. Sakl Charged

SEQUEL ...

Mr. Shapurji, munist Member of ... laterers, was ar ... Allan's Villas, ... afternoon on a ... with inciting th ... breach of the pe ...

He appeared be ... at a special sess ... Police Court yes ... was remanded on ... the undertaking ... public speeches ... in the House of ... Sir George La ... Hon. Poole, and ... after the importa ... Mr. Saklatvala ... in his seditious ... day of their trial ...

SPECIAL

Appeal to C
            Lond

An "appeal join the Metrop jary Reserve an Force in the ma order during th labour dispute" Commissioner o Police.

The appeal citizens not ex

his talk of a crushing victory over the strikers seemed heedless of the class
hostility which would result. He also overstated the extent of Communist
influence amongst both the trade union leaders and the workers. Baldwin's
calmer and less confrontational tone prevailed, and the TUC abandoned the
Strike after just over a week. Churchill was kept on the sidelines, and occupied
with producing an emergency government newspaper. He threw himself into the
task with his usual gusto, interfering and driving the staff to distraction; he wrote
much of the content, although some of his more excitable passages had to be
toned down. At its peak the circulation of the *British Gazette* reached 5 million
copies a day, and it was generally considered to have been a success. The bitter
dispute in the coal industry which had been the cause of the General Strike
dragged on for several more months, and Churchill was one of the key figures in
the cabinet's attempts to broker a settlement between the mineowners and their
workers. With the threat of 'direct action' defeated in May, Churchill typically
swung to the side of generosity and wanted to put strong pressure upon the
owners to make concessions. However the two sides were equally entrenched in
their positions, and despite much time and effort the government's efforts were
fruitless.

Churchill introduced five budgets as Chancellor, but there was little scope
for dramatic changes. His fourth budget in April 1928 introduced the first tax
on petrol, which was unpopular in rural areas and contributed to Conservative
apathy in the 1929 election. His methods of balancing the budget were often
ingenious, and he was the first Chancellor to raid the Road Fund – the revenue
from vehicle licensing – for general use. The major measure of the end of the
period was the 'de-rating' scheme, which reduced the burden of local taxation on
industry by 75% and lifted the rates from agriculture completely. The revenue lost

The Chancellor of the Exchequer
walking to the Commons to deliver
his fifth budget, 15 April 1929,
accompanied by his wife, Clementine
Churchill.
PA Photos

by local government was replaced by 'block grants' from the Treasury, a system
which expanded as the century progressed and tilted the balance of power
decisively towards the central state. Churchill worked in partnership with Neville
Chamberlain on 'de-rating', and it was integrated with the latter's extensive
reforms of the Poor Law and local government. The scheme was intended to be
the centrepiece of the government's unemployment policy and election strategy
in 1929, but it came too late to have visible effect and was too complex and dull

to make a good election weapon. His final budget in April 1929 abolished the tea duty, and also repealed an unpopular betting tax.

The Chancellor is normally the second most powerful figure in a government, but although Churchill had considerable influence in cabinet – protectionists thought far too much – he did not stand quite so high. The cabinet contained both the former Conservative leader, Austen Chamberlain, who was now restored to the fold as Foreign Secretary, and the rising figure of his half-brother Neville. Having declined the Treasury, the latter was the driving force behind the government's domestic programme. By 1929 he was widely regarded as Baldwin's probable successor – a context in which the Chancellor's name was barely mentioned. Churchill was admired and enjoyed by the party in parliament and the country, but there were too many doubts and too much baggage from his past. In fact, the changes in the cabinet which Baldwin was considering if the Conservatives won the approaching election would have included moving Churchill from the Treasury. This was not in criticism, but stemmed from the sense that he had achieved as much there as he was likely to. This was a feeling which Churchill shared, and he would not have rejected a transfer. There was no intention to drop him, and the posts considered included India, the Colonies and Agriculture. Even so, it would have been a demotion in status at least.

Churchill's career between 1916 and 1929 was shaped by his link with Lloyd George. It had taken him back into the fold in 1917 and raised him high in the post-war Coalition; it had also left him stranded after 1922, and caused him to be viewed with suspicion by many Conservatives even after his term as Chancellor of the Exchequer. When the Baldwin government was defeated in the general election of May 1929, Churchill's career seemed to have reached a natural limit. It was far from clear where he would go from here.

4

In California he was entertained by the press magnate William Randolph Hearst and the studio owner Louis Mayer, and met film stars including Charlie Chaplin.

Standing alone 1929–1940

The loss of office in 1929 left Churchill with time on his hands, and much of the next decade was to be occupied with travel and writing. Some of the former was for pleasure, and in August 1929 he departed for a three-month tour of Canada and the United States, his first visit to the continent since 1900. He was accompanied by his brother, nephew and son Randolph (then eighteen), and travelled in considerable luxury as the guest of prominent businessmen. In California he was entertained by the press magnate William Randolph Hearst and the studio owner Louis Mayer, and met film stars including Charlie Chaplin, who later visited him at Chartwell. Churchill was in New York at the time of the Wall Street Crash in October, and lost much of the earnings from his newspaper articles and books in the collapse of the stock market. For the next two years the family had to live as frugally as possible, and most of Chartwell was closed. Matters improved with a successful lecture tour of the USA in the winter of 1931–32, although this nearly resulted in his death. In the darkened evening of 31 December 1931, forgetting that traffic came from the opposite direction to that in Britain, he started across a street in the centre of New York and was knocked over by a taxi. He was severely hurt, and it was three weeks before he was able to leave hospital.

Churchill's style of living was lavish and luxurious, and Chartwell and its staff were expensive to run. Almost all of his income came from writing, and the prolific output of the following years improved the position. However, his expenditure continued unchecked, and the family finances were often verging on bankruptcy. In 1938 failed investments led to Chartwell being briefly put up for sale, but he was saved by help from one of his financier friends. Throughout the 1930s he wrote large numbers of newspaper articles which were published in Britain and America, commanding high fees. He also embarked on a series of

Previous page: Chartwell needed much
work, and Churchill found a new hobby
in bricklaying, becoming a member of
the bricklayers' trade union.
Getty Images

books, for which there were considerable advances. Soon after leaving office
he began a life of his great ancestor, the first Duke of Marlborough, which was
published in four volumes between 1933 and 1938. This was a serious enterprise,
and he engaged research assistants to gather the documents and personally
inspected the sites of the battles. He also produced a final volume of *The World
Crisis*, dealing with the Eastern Front, in 1931. The historical works sold widely
and were much admired, but a particular success was a memoir of his eventful
years up to 1900, *My Early Life*, published in 1930. There were collections of his
speeches and journalism, including the character portraits of *Great Contemporaries*
in 1937. At the end of the decade he was working on another large and ambitious
project, *A History of the English-Speaking Peoples*, for which he was paid £20,000.
By August 1939 over half a million words of this had been drafted, but the war
and then the greater priority of his wartime memoirs intervened, and it did not
appear until the later 1950s.

He wrote at Chartwell (with the first drafts being dictated), and spent
as much time there as possible. The family, staff and guests had to fit around his
schedule. He would be woken at 8.00 a.m., breakfasting in bed and remaining
there during the morning, reading newspapers and dealing with correspondence.
He took a bath before a late and substantial lunch, after which any visitors
would be proudly conducted around the estate. Churchill had a siesta in the late
afternoon, followed by a second bath and a large dinner. The most productive
part of the day came after this, working in his study into the early morning.
Churchill loved being the centre of attention and the pleasures of good living –
'my tastes are simple', he said, 'I like only the best'. The two things came together
in meals at Chartwell with his many guests – most often at lunch, as it was only
an hour's drive from central London. Churchill dominated the conversation

during these long and rich repasts; they were accompanied by vintage wines
(commonly champagne), and dinner was also followed by port and brandy.
From breakfast onwards Churchill generally had a glass of whisky at hand, but
the intake of alcohol was less than it seemed as each drink was extensively
diluted with doses of soda water and lasted for as much as two hours. His other
indulgence became a trademark: he smoked about eight Havana cigars a day.

Again, consumption was not as prodigious as it might appear. He chewed on the cigar, puffing the smoke out rather than inhaling, frequently relighting and discarding it when half-smoked. Not surprisingly, Churchill put on weight in middle age and by the mid-1930s he was about fifteen stone. He detested exercise, and attempts to diet were token and short-lived. One of the many eccentricities which made him a unique character were the tailored 'siren suits', worn for comfort whilst working at Chartwell and later 10 Downing Street; these included one in black velvet for wearing at dinner.

Churchill held court at Chartwell where the guests included the talented and successful from many walks of life. He loved company, but was too self-absorbed for friendships on anything like equal terms. The only one of this kind had been with F.E. Smith (Lord Birkenhead), who died in 1930 due to excessive drinking. Churchill enjoyed Lord Beaverbrook's mischievous company, but they differed on many issues and were not as close as they became after 1940. The rest of his immediate circle were junior followers or specialist advisors. There were three young Conservative MPs, all of whom were regarded as unscrupulous adventurers by their parliamentary colleagues and the party hierarchy. The first was Brendan Bracken, an exuberant young man with a shock of red hair who attached himself to Churchill in 1924 and became his closest and most loyal supporter. Bracken's origins were mysterious and the rumour spread that he was Churchill's illegitimate son; this was untrue, and Clementine was enraged when he failed to deny it. The two others were Robert Boothby, Churchill's aide at the Treasury from 1924 to 1929, and in the later 1930s Duncan Sandys, who married his eldest daughter, Diana. The other significant figure was older and more incongruous: teetotal and vegetarian, Professor Frederick Lindemann was a leading scientist at Oxford University. He advised Churchill on aspects of air

The three older children disappointed
and worried their parents, leading
troubled lives marked by divorce,
depression and alcoholism.

warfare in the 1930s, and became the trusted source of information on all technical matters. Churchill relied extensively on 'the Prof', giving him a peerage as Lord Cherwell in 1941 and including him as a non-departmental minister in his later cabinets.

Chartwell was a family home. Churchill was an affectionate father, inclined to indulgence, and he left discipline to Clementine. Relations within the family were often tempestuous, with angry scenes – sometimes fuelled by drink – and emotional reconciliations. The three older children disappointed and worried their parents, leading troubled lives marked by divorce, depression and alcoholism. Diana and Sarah had a difficult relationship with their mother, and both had ambitions for the stage which their parents discouraged. Less assertive and prone to depression, Diana had two failed marriages (the second to Sandys). She committed suicide in 1963, aged fifty-four. In 1936 Sarah defied her parents and eloped with a stage comedian who was nearly twice her age and had had two previous marriages. She had some successes on stage and a few film roles, and a second and troubled marriage to a London photographer which ended in divorce in 1955. By this time Sarah had a serious drinking problem, and her acting career dwindled away. Randolph caused even more concern and embarrassment, as he had many of his father's weaknesses but few of his compensating strengths. He had some talent as a speaker and writer, but lacked application and his behaviour was erratic, obstinate, arrogant and aggressive. His attempts at a political career were badly judged and flopped, but in the post-war years he had more success as a journalist and author. However, the failure to match up to his own and his father's expectations fuelled the alcoholism which led to his death in 1968, aged fifty-seven. Only the youngest child, Mary, had a stable family life. In 1947 she married Christopher Soames, later a Conservative MP and cabinet minister, and they lived not far from Chartwell; their five children were one of the pleasures of Churchill's final years.

Between 1929 and 1939 Churchill wrote, painted, travelled and worked on improving Chartwell, and his life was more varied and relaxed than it had ever been. Politics was still his greatest interest, but Churchill began to fear that the one remaining prize – the party leadership – had slipped beyond his reach. His position declined in the two years after the general election of May 1929, which brought the Labour Party into office for the second time. Churchill was not a great success on the opposition front bench, and Baldwin was not alone in thinking that he had 'made one blunder after another'. The great pressure within the Conservative Party for the adoption of a full tariff policy had the effect of pushing Churchill into the background. The slump had shaken his faith in free trade and although he was still reluctant to put duties on food imports, he was not prepared to resign from the shadow cabinet over this. However, there was little that he could say on the topic without exposing himself to criticism for inconsistency, and its prominence meant that he was largely eclipsed. There was also a demand for new faces on the Conservative front bench in place of the 'old gang' – the former ministers who were unlikely to be included in the next cabinet. Although he was only fifty-five in 1929, Churchill was included in this group. There was a feeling that he had reached his peak and that his day had passed, for in style and outlook he seemed to belong to the vanishing Victorian generation.

The direct cause of his separation from the leadership seemed to confirm that he was a remnant from the past, as Churchill emerged as the most vociferous opponent of the proposal to give the native population of India a role in its government. This issue came to the fore as his star was waning in the second half of 1930, but he was motivated by conviction rather than tactics. In November 1929 he had been deeply unhappy with Baldwin's bipartisan endorsement of the Irwin Declaration, which held out a promise of eventual dominion status. He became increasingly restive, and in September 1930 warned Baldwin that he cared about India 'more than anything else in public life'. He opposed Conservative participation in the Round Table conference which convened in London in late 1930, and was appalled when it recommended a federal constitution with areas of native control of the central government. On 26 January 1931 Baldwin committed the Conservative Party to support this plan, and next day Churchill resigned from the shadow cabinet. This was the start of the campaign which he fought for the next four-and-a-half years, with increasing intensity as the proposal moved through consultation stages to eventual legislation in the Government of India Act of 1935.

Churchill was painting at Cannes when the Labour government suddenly collapsed in the economic crisis of August 1931, to be replaced by an emergency 'National' government. This was headed by the former Labour Prime Minister, Ramsay MacDonald, and supported by the Conservative and Liberal parties and a handful of Labour MPs. Within a few weeks this had solidified into a long-term coalition of forces, and the National Government won a massive election victory in October. With 554 MPs (of whom 470 were Conservatives), its majority over the 52 Labour MPs who survived the landslide was the largest there has ever been. Although a section of the Liberal Party withdrew over the introduction of tariffs in 1932, the 'National' appeal remained strong. The government retained a substantial majority in the next general election in 1935, with 429 National MPs (of whom 387 were Conservatives) to 154 Labour and 21 independent Liberals. Churchill played no part in its formation in 1931 and was not invited to join it. This was the start of his 'wilderness years', as he did not hold office again until the outbreak of war in 1939.

There are many romantic myths and misconceptions about this period, and it is understandable that after 1945 there was a tendency to assume that the great man had been wrongfully excluded by lesser talents, with Britain languishing under 'the rule of the pygmies' – MacDonald as Prime Minister from 1931 to 1935, Baldwin from 1935 to 1937, and then Neville Chamberlain. In fact there were understandable reasons for Churchill's omission in 1931 – his standing and credibility had declined, he had little to contribute on the pressing economic and social problems, and he had quit the front bench. One of the 'old gang', he was seen as figure more of the past than the future – which his views on India only confirmed. Nor was he deliberately singled out – the Conservatives had to share the cabinet posts with the other parties, and several other former ministers were given no appointment. Churchill's position was not a factor in the making of the government, nor was it intended to isolate him. This was entirely his own doing, as he chose to go out on a limb of his own over India. His public attacks widened the breach, and he could hardly have served in an government which was firmly committed to the all-party consensus of the Round Table conference proposals.

Churchill supported the formation of the National Government in 1931, and had no quarrel with its continued existence. It was, after all, what he had always wanted: a broad-based and effective coalition against Socialism, with a moderate domestic programme. He accepted the introduction of tariffs in 1932, and supported the government across a wide range of topics throughout the decade. His criticism was confined to two areas: India and defence policy. In both cases he uttered dire warnings about lack of ministerial resolution and the perils to come, but they were approached in different ways. India came first, and played

the largest part in determining how Churchill was regarded. Between 1931
and 1935 Churchill became almost obsessive about India, pursuing a personal
crusade without restraint or care for the consequences. His methods and mistakes
marginalised him, and unfortunately India overshadowed the other theme which
began to emerge after 1932. His warnings about the danger of German aggression
and the need for rearmament were better informed and more soberly delivered,
but he had lost much of his credibility. It was the unwelcome truth that
Churchill's own mistakes of judgement and proportion were principally
responsible for his failure to attract supporters and influence policy. Doubts
about the messenger and his motives led to the discounting of his prophecies,
however powerfully they were phrased.

Churchill was passionate about the Empire and convinced that Britain's
greatness and destiny depended upon it; India was its heart, and feebleness here
would spell irreversible national decline. His conception of India had been fixed
during his service on the north-west frontier in the 1890s; he knew nothing
of most of the country or its people, and had little sense of how things had
developed in recent years. His complete rejection of a governing role for the
native population was not crudely racial, but he regarded British rule as the
natural duty of the more advanced and civilising force. This was a paternal role:
ensuring justice, order and material improvement for the whole population.
Churchill did not believe these would survive the erosion of British authority,
and he was genuinely concerned about the break up of the country into
communal religious violence and the fate of the lowest Hindu caste, the
'untouchables'; the history of the sub-continent since India became independent
in 1947 has proved these fears to have been far from unreasonable. He had no
time for the Indian middle-class nationalist politicians, whom he considered

Opposite: The notes for Churchill's
speech in the House of Commons
warning of the danger from a rearming
Germany, 28 November 1934.
Curtis Brown/Churchill Archives Centre
CHAR 9/108/B

represented no one but themselves, and some of his strongest language was used
in denunciations of Gandhi. Churchill was also concerned about the effects of
Indian self-government upon Britain and the trade upon which the feeding of
the domestic population depended. He regarded constitutional change in India as
needless folly which would undermine Britain's position in the world. It was an
abdication of the will to govern, and he looked to the Conservative Party to give
the lion's roar and assert itself against it.

The campaign to persuade the Conservative Party to reject the India
reforms was fought in two arenas: the voluntary membership and the
parliamentary party. The rebels came closest to success in the first of these, but
the leadership's position was endorsed at the party's Central Council and annual
conference meetings in 1933 and 1934 – although sometimes only narrowly.
Many Conservatives were dubious about Baldwin's bipartisan line but supported
it through loyalty, the need to maintain party unity, and the lack of a credible
alternative. Churchill conspicuously failed to provide this: he did not command
confidence, and his standpoint was a purely negative one. His views were
impractical and outdated, and he failed to recognise the commitments that had
been made by previous governments – including those in which he had served.
In March 1931 Baldwin rebuffed Churchill's attack by quoting his endorsement
of reform in 1919–21, and it was hard for Churchill to seem consistent or
convincing. He seemed to have swung wildly to the extreme, with violent
and provocative language: Congress was to be crushed, negotiations would be
'monstrous', the policy was a 'crime' and it results would be 'catastrophe'. Some
felt that he had lost his reason and was reacting purely emotionally, whilst others
regarded it as a desperate and unprincipled attempt to smash the government and
seize the leadership.

H/C 28.11.34 (141)

I, (The Danger)

To urge preprns defence
not to assert imminence war.

On contrary if war were imminent
preprn wd. be too late.

Do not believe war imminent
nor inevitable,

but if we do not begin forthwith
put ourselves in posn. security
will soon be beyond
our power do so.

What is gt. new fact
wh. has broken upon us last 18 mths?

(Germany rearming.)

There is event wh. rivets attention Europe
and affects thoughts every country,
throws all other issues in backgrnd.

Germany rearming!

She has already powerful well-eqpd. army
w. excellent artillery
and immense reserves armed, trained men.

German munition factories
working practically under war condns
war material pouring fr. them
ever broadening flow.

All this direct breach of Peace Treaty.

Germany rearming on land, some extent at sea
but it is (Air) armaments of Germany
wh. most urgently concern us.

83

Churchill fought a sustained campaign in parliament, but his 'rogue elephant' methods meant that he had no significant allies and few supporters. His wild onslaughts made it difficult for other senior figures who had doubts to work with him, and consolidated moderate opinion behind Baldwin. His support was limited to about eighty 'die-hard' MPs, and many of these were uncomfortable with Churchill's previous career and reluctant to regard him as their leader. In any case, the number was too few: nearly four hundred Conservative MPs remained loyal, and the government had substantial majorities on every key vote. At several critical points Churchill lost momentum due to tactical mistakes. In March 1933 his speech in the debate on the White Paper was wrecked by an unproven allegation that the government was coercing the Indian Civil Service. The most damage was done by the failure of his accusation in April 1934 that the India Secretary, Sir Samuel Hoare, and Lord Derby had improperly influenced the Manchester Chamber of Commerce (a key body due to the importance of Lancashire's cotton exports to India) to alter its submission to the Select Committee. Churchill was not far from the mark, but his evidence was inconclusive and the charges were rejected when the Committee of Privileges reported in June. He took this badly and his stock slumped even further – it looked like a malicious personal attack on Hoare, showing that he would stoop to any depths. In January 1935 his son Randolph stood as a rebel candidate at a by-election in the Liverpool constituency of Wavertree, dividing the Conservative vote and losing the seat. Churchill had been against this but could not refuse to speak in his support, and was the target of most of the blame afterwards. In the following month the bill passed its crucial second reading with only eighty-four Conservative MPs voting against, and it became law as the Government of India Act in June 1935, giving a more significant role to native Indians.

Accepting his defeat, Churchill turned to his other concern – the danger from Germany. He had begun to warn of Germany's rearmament and intentions in 1932, even before Hitler's rise to power, and when the Nazis took control in 1933 he was swift to recognize the aggressive and expansionist nature of their regime. Churchill wanted any revisions to the discredited Versailles peace settlement to be considered from a position of strength. This meant that Britain's security depended upon firm diplomacy backed up by adequate rearmament programmes, especially in the air. There was a general fear that a future war would begin with the bombing of civilian populations on a massive scale, and so the existence of a German air force – banned under the Versailles treaty – caused alarm. It was understood that the only defence was the possession of an equally powerful air force as a deterrent, but it was difficult to assess what strength was needed. The National Government began a programme of limited rearmament in 1934, and this was increased in stages as the international situation deteriorated during the next few years. However, for Churchill this was too little and too late, and he believed that Britain was lagging dangerously behind. The government's other approach was the policy of 'appeasement', settling grievances in a conciliatory manner; to Churchill, this seemed to be a policy of irresolution and weakness, which would only encourage the restless power to return with demands for more. At first, with the economic depression and a public opinion dominated by the memory of the First World War, Churchill seemed to be exaggerating the peril. Once again there were doubts about his judgement and intentions, but in May 1935 he seemed to be vindicated by German statements that the *Luftwaffe* was larger than the Royal Air Force. Baldwin had promised that Britain would not be overtaken when replying to Churchill's warnings in March 1934, and was now left in the humiliating position of apologising to the House of Commons.

Churchill had seemed wild and emotional over India, but was sober and well-informed about rearmament. He had a semi-official position as a member of the government's Air Defence Research Committee from 1935, but this was not the main source of his information. He had a wide range of contacts, and a number of middle-ranking officers, diplomats and civil servants who were disturbed by the complacency of their superiors passed confidential information to Churchill. The most important of these were Ralph Wigram of the Foreign Office and a neighbour of Churchill's, Desmond Morton. He was the Director of the Industrial Intelligence Centre, which had the task of assessing German manufacturing capacity and monitoring the level of rearmament. The result was that Churchill seemed to have a better grasp of the position than government ministers, and his speeches were listened to in a way in which the fulminations on India were not. As the position grew more gloomy, Churchill's consistency and foresight stood out in splendid isolation from the mistakes and muddles of the government, and his stature grew. However, he still lacked support and was distrusted by many Conservative MPs, whilst until 1939 the Labour opposition denounced him as a right-wing 'warmonger'.

Churchill would have been more successful if his tactics had been better judged. He was a remote and unpopular figure in the Commons for most of the 1930s, where his habit of attending only when he was delivering an Olympian pronouncement was resented. The rifts caused by the India campaign were deeper than Churchill rather naively expected, and his hopes of returning to the cabinet between 1935 and 1937 were unrealistic. The fear that he would be a disruptive force in the cabinet was too strong, whilst his inclusion would send a hostile signal to Germany. His small personal clique inspired little confidence, and when a group of Conservative critics of appeasement emerged they kept a

The greater degree of authority which Churchill built up from the spring of 1936 was squandered by his disastrous intervention in support of King Edward VIII during the abdication crisis at the end of the year.

distance from Churchill, preferring to look to Amery or Eden for leadership. The greater degree of authority which Churchill built up from the spring of 1936 was squandered by his disastrous intervention in support of King Edward VIII during the abdication crisis at the end of the year. Churchill revered the institution of the monarchy as an important part of Britain's historic identity, and considered it a valuable bulwark against dictatorship. He feared that the unprecedented step of an abdication would weaken it and wanted Edward to remain, mistakenly assuming that the King's passion for Mrs Simpson would not last. Churchill's personal sympathy for Edward and his romantic loyalty to the crown led to his plea for more time to explore other solutions. In the brief but intense crisis, his motives were misunderstood and he was widely suspected of seeking to bring the government down. He ignored advice, acted rashly and alienated those who had begun to support him on other issues. In a shattering reverse, Churchill was howled down when he tried to speak in the House of Commons at the height of the crisis on 7 December 1936. He was humiliated and had to abandon his speech, and for a brief interval believed that his political career was finished. All the doubts about his judgement were reinforced and, although he recovered some ground with a tactful and conciliatory speech three days later, he kept a lower profile during most of 1937.

In May 1937 Churchill seconded the election of Neville Chamberlain as leader of the Conservative Party, but his hopes of office under the new Prime Minister were disappointed. He was restrained in his comments for the rest of that year, mainly confining his suggestions and criticisms to private correspondence. However, the crises of 1938 led to the most serious and public clashes between Churchill and the government. Dismayed by Eden's resignation as Foreign Secretary in February 1938 and Hitler's *Anschluss* with Austria in the

Opposite: As appeasement failed in 1939, Churchill's stock rose: Strube's cartoon for the *Daily Express* on 6 July 1939 shows the press calling for his inclusion in the Cabinet, and Prime Minister Neville Chamberlain's reluctance.
The British Library, Newspaper Library

following month, Churchill returned to public warnings. His denunciation of the Munich Agreement of October 1938, which appeased Hitler's demands for parts of Czechoslovakia, as 'a total and unmitigated defeat' ran counter to the euphoric relief of the public that war had been avoided. Churchill and the handful of Conservative 'anti-appeasers' were isolated and under pressure during the months between Munich and the German occupation of Prague in March 1939. The atmosphere became bitter, and an open breach and resignation of the whip seemed possible after Churchill's speech in the Munich debate, and his vote with Labour on 17 November 1938 on the question of establishing a Ministry of Supply to hasten rearmament. There was criticism in the branches of his constituency association at Epping, although with the support of his chairman this was contained. Rebuffed within the Conservative Party, Churchill sought to open contacts with Liberal and Labour politicians. He also began to advocate an alliance with Russia, a pragmatic softening of his anti-Soviet position which also made him more acceptable to the left-wing critics of appeasement.

Hitler's repudiation of the Munich settlement by occupying the rest of the Czech lands in March 1939 was a devastating blow to appeasement. It demonstrated that Hitler could not be trusted and suggested that there was no limit to his aggressive plans; Chamberlain seemed to have been weak and foolish, whilst events had confirmed Churchill's wisdom. There was a dramatic change in Churchill's public standing during the following months, including a press campaign in the summer of 1939 for his return to the cabinet. Chamberlain resisted this, but the downwards slide towards war in the Polish crisis made continued exclusion impossible. Chamberlain's last efforts at appeasement failed, and when war was declared on 3 September 1939 Churchill was offered the position of First Lord of the Admiralty and a place in the inner War Cabinet.

His return to office was a triumph over adversity, and his position was in many ways independent of the rest of the government. Over the following months they became increasingly blamed for inadequacies in preparation, whilst Churchill's stock rose further. He was untarnished by the failure of appeasement, and could not be blamed for the lack of armaments. Doubts about his judgement during the First World War were displaced by growing confidence, stimulated by his determination, vigour, martial spirit and belief in victory.

At the start of hostilities Churchill was once again where he had been in 1914, in charge of the navy. The signal 'Winston is back' was flashed to British fleets and warships around the world, and it was a sign of how differently he was now regarded that this would raise morale rather than lower it. It was Churchill's good fortune that the activities of the navy stood out during the months of the 'phoney war', as the public waited uneasily for air assaults and land battles which failed to materialise. The Royal Navy had an overwhelming superiority over the

German fleet on the surface, but it was stretched to cover Britain's worldwide commitments and protect the trade routes. There were no major battles, but some successes which showed the valour against odds and boldness of the 'Nelson spirit' which had seemed to be lacking in the First World War. The German 'pocket battleship' *Graf Spee* was trapped in South American waters by British cruisers and had to be ignominiously scuttled, whilst a daring raid on the supply ship *Altmark* in Norwegian waters freed the prisoners which it had taken. German submarines proved to be more of a problem, although they were still too few to make serious inroads into merchant shipping and the convoy system was introduced from the start of the war. However, early in the war the aircraft carrier *Courageous* was lost and a daring raid into the main British anchorage of Scapa Flow sank the battleship *Royal Oak* at its moorings, both with heavy casualties. Despite these setbacks, Churchill's fortitude and determination ensured that service and public confidence remained high.

Unlike other ministers, he seemed eager to take the war to the enemy. Although he still trod on his colleagues' toes with his proposals, he was less pushy and more experienced than he had been in 1914. Churchill's growing authority was shown by his appointment on 8 April 1940 as chairman of a new Military Co-ordinating Committee. This consisted of the ministers and chiefs-of-staff of the Army, Navy and Air Force, and was intended to harmonise planning and strategy. However, the problems in the central direction of the war were exposed almost immediately by the lightning German invasion of Denmark and Norway. Despite some naval successes at Narvik, the British response was a fiasco, with visible deficiencies in planning and combined operations and a fatal lack of air cover. Churchill had considerable responsibility during the Norwegian campaign, and accepted this when the House of Commons debated it on 7 and 8 May

When war broke out, Churchill was offered the post he had also held in 1914. His return to the Admiralty in September 1939 was commemorated a decade later on the cover of the popular magazine *Picture Post*.
Getty Images

1940. However, the issue had now become the complacency and competence of the Prime Minister. Although the government won the vote, the withdrawal of support by around eighty MPs fatally weakened Chamberlain's position. It was clear that the Labour Party would not join a Coalition under his leadership, and on 9 May Chamberlain reluctantly accepted that he would have to resign. There were only two possible successors: Churchill and the Earl of Halifax, the Foreign Secretary since 1938. There was support for Halifax in both parties; it was certainly possible for the Prime Minister to be in the House of Lords (the last occasion had been in 1902), but he would have had to rely upon Churchill in the House of Commons. At the crucial meeting on the afternoon of 9 May, Churchill remained silent and did not offer to serve under Halifax. After a few moments – and with some relief – Halifax declined the premiership, and Churchill's appointment became inevitable. Shortly after 6 p.m. on 10 May, Churchill saw King George VI at Buckingham Palace and became Prime Minister of a new Coalition government which included the Labour Party. Early that morning the Allies had again been taken by surprise as the German invasion of the Low Countries and France began, and the nature of the war abruptly changed.

5

Walking with destiny 1940–1945

In May 1940 Churchill had at last reached the top, although by an unusual route and in extraordinary circumstances. He was sixty-five years old, and had never expected to have to wait so long. During the years in the wilderness in the 1930s his career had seemed to be over, but now the image of the lone prophet was his greatest asset. He owed his position to no one else, and this enhanced his authority and public standing. He was not regarded as a party politician, but as a great individualist whose moment had now come. The chance to be the nation's saviour appealed powerfully to Churchill's romantic imagination and his sense of history. In his memoirs he recalled that when he became Prime Minister, 'I felt as if I were walking with destiny, and that all my past life had been but a preparation for this hour and for this trial'. In many ways this was true, for Churchill had a unique breadth of experience in British politics and government, and was the only figure in the cabinet to have held high office during the previous world war. His particular expertise in military matters meant that there was little objection when he assumed the position of Minister of Defence as well. This was a new post, subordinating the previously independent ministries for the three armed services, and it gave Churchill unrivalled command of the strategic direction of the war. The service ministers still remained, but were outside the War Cabinet and dealt with the execution of its decisions and the more routine administration.

Churchill concentrated his attention upon the conduct of the war and the crucial questions of relations with allied powers and the key neutral states. The domestic scene was left mainly to others, with Labour leaders taking charge of several key ministries – in particular, the powerful trade union leader Ernest Bevin oversaw the allocation of manpower as Minister of Labour. Like Lloyd George, Churchill was fond of bringing successful businessmen and outside experts into key positions, especially to deal with the problems of organising war

ALL BEHIND YOU, WINSTON (Copyright in All Countries.)

production. The small War Cabinet included Clement Attlee, the Labour Party
leader and Deputy Prime Minister, and one or two other Labour figures.
For the first few months of his premiership Churchill relied heavily upon
Neville Chamberlain, who accepted office as Lord President of the Council.
The continuation of Halifax as Foreign Secretary and Chamberlain's loyal
support strengthened Churchill's position and reassured the mainstream of
the Conservative Party that it had not fallen into the hands of mavericks and
adventurers. However, Churchill also valued Chamberlain's administrative abilities
and gave him a key role in co-ordinating home affairs. The rising tide of public
resentment against the 'guilty men' responsible for the failures of appeasement
and rearmament weakened the position of Chamberlain and the other pre-war
ministers, but Churchill was genuinely sorry when illness forced Chamberlain to
resign in the autumn of 1940. Some of the 'appeasers' had been left out in May
1940, and public hostility to them helped Churchill change the balance in his
cabinet. In December 1940 he persuaded Halifax to become Ambassador to the
United States, and Anthony Eden replaced him as Foreign Secretary. Apart from
Eden, Churchill relied upon his pre-war circle of cronies, and in particular upon
Beaverbrook, Bracken and Lindemann. The Churchill Coalition combined the
conventional political parties with a collection of diverse individuals. Although
positions could rise and fall, and there was need for frequent reshuffles, as the
war progressed they became an effective team who worked mainly in a non-party
atmosphere.

From the outset there was no doubt as to who was in charge, and
Churchill's authority was rarely questioned. At first this was because there was no
time for dissent to appear, as the German *blitzkrieg* shattered the French armies
and drove the British Expeditionary Force back to the Channel ports. Churchill

made several visits to Paris in the hope of stiffening French resolve, but decided against committing further British forces – especially precious fighter aircraft. A pause in the German advance allowed the evacuation of 224,318 British and 111,172 French troops from the beaches of Dunkirk, salvaging something from the disaster. After this Hitler swiftly completed his triumph, and France sued for peace on 17 June. Britain now stood alone and vulnerable, with an outnumbered air force and an army which had had to abandon most of its equipment in France. The War Cabinet briefly considered the possibility of a compromise peace, but there was little opposition to Churchill's determination to fight on.

In public, he was forceful and frank about what lay ahead. He prized honesty and was confident of public resilience, telling the House of Commons in October 1940 that 'our people do not mind being told the worst'. His first speech as Prime Minister, on 13 May, had struck a new note of realism and determination, with its promise of 'blood, toil, tears and sweat' as the way to 'victory however long and hard the road may be'. Churchill's speeches in the Commons were widely reported, but it was his radio broadcasts which had the greatest impact. Although there were only five of these during this vital period, they conveyed his vigour, steadied morale and imparted confidence. On 4 June, after Dunkirk, he did not offer excuses but defiance:

We shall go on to the end … we shall defend our Island, whatever the cost may be, we shall fight on the beaches, we shall fight on the landing grounds, we shall fight in the fields and the streets, we shall fight in the hills; we shall never surrender.

There was more at stake than just survival, and Churchill constantly presented Britain as the defender of freedom, tolerance and justice against the forces of tyranny, oppression and slavery. There was no shadow of doubt about the rightness or importance of the cause: it was not a conflict between nations, but a struggle against evil. This was the test that the British people faced, standing alone but not only for themselves. Following the surrender of France, Churchill's short two-minute broadcast on 18 June summed up what the war was being fought for:

Hitler knows that he will have to break us in this Island or lose the war. If we can stand up to him, all Europe may be free and the life of the world may move forward into broad, sunlit uplands. But if we fail, then the whole world, including the United States, including all that we have known or cared for, will sink into the abyss of a new Dark Age … Let us therefore brace ourselves to our duties, and so bear ourselves that if the British Empire and its Commonwealth last for a thousand years men will still say, 'This was their finest hour'.

The atmosphere of steadiness and fortitude in the face of possible invasion was not created by Churchill out of nothing, but his moving language strengthened these currents in public opinion and made them predominant. There was of course anxiety and pessimism, but Churchill built a consensus which held these distractions at bay and directed the energy of the nation into constructive effort. For the first time, there was harmony between Churchill's view of himself and that held by the mass of the people. He became the personification of the nation's resolution, a British bulldog in spirit and image – an aspect emphasised by the thrust of his jaw and his expression in public appearances, photographs and posters. Instantly recognisable in person or on the cinema newsreels, he was a distinctive figure with his variety of hats, his walking stick, the perennial cigar and the spotted bow ties worn with formal dress; he also had a range of uniforms and the comfortable siren suits for military occasions, travel and conferences. His famous two-finger 'V sign' was widely adopted; it stood for 'Victory' but was in reality a symbol of endurance, of the belief in winning through despite the odds.

In the summer and autumn of 1940, Churchill's determined leadership and inspiring oratory made a crucial contribution at the moment of greatest peril. Britain's continued resistance between June 1940 and May 1941 prevented Hitler from achieving victory, and Churchill's significance as a major figure in world history rests upon this most of all.

During this period Britain was threatened by invasion, its cities were subjected to heavy bombing, its supplies of food and raw materials were besieged by German submarines, and its vital strategic position in north Africa was imperilled. The pressures were intense, and brought out both the best and the worst in Churchill. The best was his resilience and purposeful leadership, and the maintenance of public visibility with a constant round of visits to bomb-damaged areas and military inspections. The worst was the often unreasonable demands he placed on those working with him, and a tendency to bully or lose his temper. He often expected more of his military commanders than could be managed with the limited resources at their disposal, and when he lost confidence in their drive he could be brutal about replacing them. However, although this might sometimes have been unfair, being a good butcher was a vital part of his task; he

British aircraft in the Battle of Britain were fewer in number but superior in performance to the German fighters: a Spitfire and a Hurricane (in foreground) patrol the southern coastline in the Second World War.
Getty Images

was rarely capricious, and as British fortunes improved he stuck with the commanders who had demonstrated their effectiveness, even if – like Montgomery – they were sometimes difficult to manage.

On 18 June 1940 Churchill warned the nation that the 'battle of France' was over and the 'battle of Britain' was about to begin. The army was desperately being re-equipped, and a force of older part-time volunteers, the 'Home Guard', was raised to assist it. However, the feasibility of invasion by Germany depended upon their securing control of the skies, for without this any seaborne force would be vulnerable to attack from the air and from surface warships. The Royal Air Force was outnumbered, and although its Spitfire fighters were more advanced than their *Luftwaffe* opponents, both machines and trained pilots were in short supply. Churchill tackled the first problem by sending his friend, the businessman and maverick newspaper-owner Lord Beaverbrook, to head a new Ministry of Aircraft Production. Beaverbrook knew how desperate the position was, and in a whirlwind of activity he boosted the flow from the factories. This took a little time to feed through to the front line, but as the aerial battle continued it was shortage of pilots that became the graver problem. Fortunately most of the combat took place over the fields of south-east England,

and British pilots who managed to escape from damaged aircraft landed in friendly territory and could fly again. The new invention of radar also played a crucial role by giving sufficient warning of German attacks for the fighters to intercept them. As the battle developed during August, the RAF was able to hold its own and inflict heavier casualties on the enemy. The German switch in September to attacking London gave a vital respite to the fighter bases (the previous target), whilst the greater distance exposed the German bombers for a longer period. The civilian population suffered, but the effectiveness of the RAF and the onset of autumn weather led Hitler to abandon the plans for invasion. He never seriously contemplated it again, although Britain could not feel entirely free from the danger for another year. Churchill captured this pivotal moment in one of his most memorable phrases, declaring on 20 August 1940 – whilst the battle still raged – that 'Never in the field of human conflict was so much owed by so many to so few'.

By the autumn of 1940 Churchill had acquired a commanding stature and an unprecedented level of public support, silencing the critics and doubters. When Neville Chamberlain's health collapsed in September with the swift onset of cancer, Churchill was the only possible choice to succeed him as Conservative leader. Clementine was strongly opposed to this step, believing that it would diminish her husband's national appeal, but he remembered Lloyd George's vulnerability during and after the First World War. Churchill could hardly have allowed someone else to take such a potentially powerful position, and he was formally elected Leader of the Conservative Party on 9 October, without opposition. This strong political base made his position more secure, although for the duration of the war Churchill gave scant attention to considerations of party politics. He had little need to do so, for from the autumn of 1940 he stood far

above any other political figure in public estimation. The twenty-five radio broadcasts which he made between May 1940 and December 1941 were heard on average by 70% of the population, and he enjoyed consistently high approval ratings of around 75–80% throughout the war. Churchill had tapped a well of public confidence which never ran dry, and it was accepted by both the public and other politicians that he was the one essential and irreplaceable figure in the government. This did not mean that he was immune to criticism, and the government and other ministers were sometimes much more unpopular than he was. There were a few moments of setback and crisis when Churchill's position looked more vulnerable than it actually was, but no serious challenge ever materialised because the public would never have supported it. Churchill was regarded with affection and trust, and there was confidence in his indomitable will and single-minded pursuit of victory; he may have become a party leader, but he was never seen as being another party politician.

For much of the war the Churchills lived not in 10 Downing Street itself but in 'the Annexe', a building nearby on Whitehall. This was strengthened against bomb damage, and beneath it were the underground Cabinet War Rooms

where Winston spent most of his time. He had his own office and bedroom, and the cabinet and service chiefs could meet here in safety regardless of air raids. It was cramped and busy, but Churchill ran the war effort through the staff and communications at his disposal here. Churchill's daily routine was similar to that of peacetime, and put considerable pressure upon his staff and senior officers. They were expected to adapt to 'Winston time', and to be available when needed, especially late at night. The Prime Minister was normally woken at 8.00 a.m. for the daily digest of reports on the war situation, and would work in bed during the morning, issuing instructions through his aides. He would rise if there was a War Cabinet or committee meeting in the morning, and took a hot bath before lunch. There would be more meetings or discussions in the afternoon, but Churchill always insisted on taking a nap of at least an hour at some point in the late afternoon, even if this meant keeping people waiting. He was able to go to sleep at once and would emerge reinvigorated; these siestas played a crucial part in sustaining him through a working week averaging ninety hours, and in keeping him mentally as well as physically fresh. Churchill took a large dinner at about 8.00 p.m., at which there would be staff and guests and the conversation would still be focused upon the war. After this he would work into the early hours, sometimes not retiring until 3.00 a.m. This routine was made possible by his vigour and physical robustness, and he had relatively few serious health problems. Throughout the war Churchill travelled extensively, to and from conferences or visiting the theatres of war. He was conveyed sometimes by battleship and twice on the liner *Queen Mary*; these large ships were relatively comfortable, and their speed made them difficult for U-boats to intercept. His other journeys were by air, in flying boats or hastily adapted bombers. The latter could be noisy, rough and cold – the long trip to Moscow in 1942 being particularly gruelling. Clementine gave him much support but did not usually travel with him overseas; when not looking after the household, she was engaged in war-related charity work, in particular the Red Cross Aid to Russia Fund.

Churchill had great powers of concentration and would have bursts of energy, although he could get tired and grumpy. In these moods, when the saving grace of his usual good humour was absent, he could be abrasive, aggressive, stubborn and childish. Such tempests usually passed swiftly, but they added to the stress and exhaustion of those around him. It was understood that he did not mean it personally, and that his irascibility and impatience were the result of frustration and total commitment to the war effort. Clementine would intervene when his behaviour became particularly boorish, and matters would improve for a while at least. The pressure was greatest upon the Chiefs of Staff of the three armed services, but they generally accepted it as a part of the price for Churchill's unique talents, drive and inspirational leadership – for that indefinable quality of 'genius' that marked him out. Churchill governed the war effort through key

HOLDING THE LINE!

committees, despatches to commanders in the field, and a constant flow of minutes, enquiries and instructions. Most famous were the red labels with the instruction 'Action this Day' which were attached to the minutes that required an immediate response. He galvanised the administrative machine, sweeping aside bureaucracy and muddle, and insisted upon clear and concise summaries on every topic. He enquired into every difficulty and shortage, and his energy was transmitted down through the ranks.

With a touch of humour, Churchill summed up his approach in his memoirs: 'All I wanted was compliance with my wishes after reasonable discussion.' In fact, he had to work with and through others; his executive authority was considerable, but still much less than that of Hitler, Stalin or even Roosevelt. The War Cabinet dealt with the broader political and strategic issues, and – as Minister of Defence – Churchill also chaired the Defence Committee (Operations) which oversaw the military conduct of the war. The service Chiefs of Staff were members of the latter, and Churchill dealt with them directly and also through the mediation of his military secretary, General 'Pug' Ismay, who served throughout the war. Apart from Ismay, the senior officer in most frequent contact with Churchill was General Sir Alan Brooke, who from late 1941 until the end of the war headed the army as Chief of the Imperial General Staff (CIGS) and was chairman of the three-man Chiefs of Staff Committee. It was his task in particular to cope with the Prime Minister's flow of instructions and ideas. The latter were a characteristic Churchill feature: in Brooke's slightly jaundiced view, 'Winston had ten ideas every day, only one of which was good, and he did not know which it was.'

Churchill's fertile imagination ranged across every aspect of the war, and it could take a wearing amount of time and energy to dissuade him from the more impracticable suggestions. However, some ideas were innovative and might otherwise have been neglected, such as Churchill's grasp in 1942 that a floating pre-fabricated harbour would be needed for any invasion of France, which led to the development of crucially successful 'Mulberry' harbours used after the D-day landings. Churchill was always interested in applying science to warfare and in new weapons and tactics, and this led amongst other things to the development of radar, the atomic bomb, anti-submarine devices, night air-navigation systems, the limpet mine and PIAT (the Personal Infantry Anti-Tank weapon). He gave Lindemann a wide remit as his expert adviser, and also put him in charge of the Statistical Section. This was another innovation, and its small staff provided Churchill with clear and reliable data, especially upon war production. Churchill was also very receptive to signals intelligence, especially from the Government Communications HQ at Bletchley Park, where the crucial German 'Enigma' codes had been broken. He called this 'the goose that laid golden eggs' and demanded to see the decrypts directly, obtaining them before the Chiefs of Staff and using them to support his arguments. Finally, Churchill was always attracted to 'cloak and dagger' and supported the work of the Special Operations Executive: its commando raids and encouragement of resistance in occupied

Europe were particularly useful in maintaining morale during the middle years of the war.

The most difficult period was the year between the fall of France and the German invasion of Russia in June 1941. The French warships based in north Africa were a particular problem, for Britain's naval superiority would be in danger if they were ordered home and fell into German hands. In a decision of ruthless self-preservation, in July 1940 Churchill ordered that the ships were made harmless; some units resisted, and the bloodshed that followed was condemned in France. The conflict spread to the Mediterranean and north Africa after Italy entered the war on 10 June 1940. In September the Italian forces in Libya invaded Egypt, threatening the Suez Canal; the supply routes through the Mediterranean were closed, and the strategic base of Malta besieged from the air. In October 1940 Mussolini attacked Greece but suffered defeats, and in January 1941 British forces under General Wavell made a successful counter-attack in north Africa and pushed into Libya. These gains were lost in the spring and summer of 1941, when German forces crushed the Greek resistance. British troops diverted to Greece had to be evacuated, and at the same time the victories of the innovative German commander Rommel in the Libyan desert forced Wavell into retreat. Churchill considered him to be too cautious and dismissed him from the Middle East command in June 1941, although he later appointed him Viceroy of India in 1943. Throughout this period the heavy night-time bombing of British cities known as the 'Blitz' continued, with a renewed wave of attacks in the spring of 1941. Churchill's private slogan during these months was 'We must just KBO', which stood for 'keep buggering on'.

A major concern during the period of standing alone was that Britain was exhausting its financial resources and would become unable to draw on the

manufacturing power of the United States. It was essential to secure material
assistance, but America was still in isolationist mood and President Roosevelt had
to tread carefully until he had secured re-election in November 1940. One of
Churchill's most important contributions was the working relationship which he
established with the US President. This began shortly after Churchill's return to
the Admiralty, with a letter from Roosevelt in mid-September 1939 indicating
his concern about the European war and inviting Churchill to inform him of
'anything you want me to know about'. Roosevelt's overture was private and
did not commit him to anything, but Churchill saw the potential and responded
promptly and positively. Recognising the informality of this unusual exchange,
he signed his reply 'Former Naval Person' – a reference to the link that
they had both held offices related to their navies in the last war. So began
a correspondence which became even more important after Churchill became
Prime Minister, amounting to nearly 2,000 letters by Roosevelt's death in 1945.
They also talked by telephone when matters were urgent, and met face-to-face
nine times during the war. Both leaders were naturally concerned to safeguard
their own national interests, but this closeness at the highest level was important.
It was certainly a 'special relationship', even though it was not an equal one.
Britain's vulnerable position in 1940–41 meant that Churchill's need was the
greater, and he took special care to foster the link and encourage American
assistance. After entering the war, the scale of American power eclipsed Britain,
and Churchill found himself the junior partner. Even so, he was always listened
to with respect, and got his way more often than Britain's material contributions
might otherwise have justified. Although there were some frictions – especially
over Britain's imperial role – they were far less than might have been expected.
The unusually close co-operation in planning, intelligence and the conduct of

MOST SECRET. Copy No.

TELEGRAMS AND LETTERS EXCHANGED BETWEEN THE NAVAL PERSON AND PRESIDENT ROOSEVELT

11TH SEPTEMBER, 1939—7TH MAY, 1940

Letter from President Roosevelt to Mr. Churchill dated 11.9.39.

My dear Churchill,

It is because you and I occupied similar positions in the World War that I want you to know how glad I am that you are back again in the Admiralty. Your problems are, I realise, complicated by new factors but the essential is not very different. What I want you and the Prime Minister to know is that I shall at all times welcome it if you will keep me in touch personally with anything you want me to know about. You can always send sealed letters through your pouch or my pouch.

I am glad you did the Marlboro volumes before this thing started—and I much enjoyed reading them.

With my sincere regards,
Faithfully yours,
FRANKLIN D. ROOSEVELT.

The substance of the following message was communicated to the President by Mr. Churchill in a telephone conversation on the 5th October, 1939 :—

"*Iroquois* is probably a thousand miles West of Ireland. Presume you could not meet her before 50th meridian. There remains about a thousand miles in which outrage might be committed. U-boat danger inconceivable in these broad waters. Only method can be time-bomb planted at Queenstown. We think this not impossible.

Am convinced full exposure of all facts known to United States Government, including sources of information, especially if official, only way of frustrating plot. Action seems urgent. Presume you have warned *Iroquois* to search ship."

NAVAL PERSON *to* PRESIDENT ROOSEVELT. 5.10.39.

We quite understand natural desire of United States to keep belligerent acts out of their waters. We like the idea of a wide limit of, say, 300 miles within which no submarines of any belligerent country should act. If America requests all belligerents to comply, we should immediately declare that we should respect your wishes. General questions of International Law would, of course, remain unprejudiced. More difficulty arises about surface ships, because if a raider operates from or takes refuge in the American zone, we should have to be protected or allowed to protect ourselves. We have mentioned several other instances to Mr. Kennedy. We do not mind how far south the prohibited zone goes, provided that it is effectively maintained. We should have great difficulty in accepting a zone which was only policed by some weak neutral. But, of course, if the American Navy takes care of it, that is all right.

Thirdly, we are still not sure whether raider off Brazil is *Scheer* or *Hipper*, but widespread movements are being made by us to meet either case. The more American ships cruising along the South American coast the better, as you, Sir, would no doubt hear what they saw or did not see. Raider might then find American waters rather crowded, or may anyhow prefer to go on to South African trade-route, where we are preparing.

We wish to help you in every way in keeping the war out of American waters.

Opposite: The American Ambassador in
London relays Roosevelt's message
announcing the US entry into the war
on 8 December 1941, the day after the
Japanese attack on Pearl Harbor.
Churchill signed his messages to

Roosevelt as 'Former Naval Person',
a reference to both leaders' past
connection with their country's navy.
Chartwell Trust/Churchill Archives Centre,
CHAR 20/46/53

operations which characterised the Anglo-American war effort flowed from the tone set at the top.

The first fruits of this partnership came whilst the United States was still neutral, when in the summer of 1940 Britain traded bases in the Caribbean for fifty American destroyers; although elderly, they were more than suitable for escorting the Atlantic convoys. Much more important was Lend-Lease, which became law in March 1941 and lasted until the defeat of Germany. Britain could now secure all the supplies and munitions that it needed; the orders placed stimulated the American economy, but even so Churchill correctly acknowledged the uniqueness of the gesture when he called this 'the most unsordid act'. The relief from financial anxiety and the sense of purpose that followed was reflected in Churchill's declaration in a broadcast on 9 February 1941: 'Give us the tools, and we will finish the job'. Unrestricted German submarine warfare led to American assistance with convoy protection in the western Atlantic, easing the burden on the Royal Navy. As the United States was drawn closer to involvement, Churchill and Roosevelt met for the first time at Placentia Bay on the coast of Newfoundland on 9–10 August 1941. They both travelled by battleship and exchanged visits to each other's vessel, but whilst the location was secret the result was not. This was the 'Atlantic Charter', a statement of principles and freedoms upon which the two countries agreed; it affirmed a common purpose, although it did not commit the United States to entering the war. However, the partial involvement which already existed led Hitler to declare war upon the United States after Japan's attack on Pearl Harbor in December 1941. When he heard of these two developments, Churchill concluded simply that 'we had won the war' – it was now just a matter of time and effort.

The other crucial development had occurred six months previously, when

COPY.

EMBASSY OF THE UNITED STATES OF
AMERICA.

IAL No. T 946

London,
December 8, 1941.

Dear Prime Minister,

I am very happy to send this message to you:

"FOR THE FORMER NAVAL PERSON FROM THE PRESIDENT:

"The Senate passed the all-out declaration of war

82 to nothing, and the House has passed it 382 to 1.   Today

all of us are in the same boat with you and the people of

the Empire and it is a ship which will not and can not be

sunk".

Sincerely,

(Sgd) JOHN G. WINANT.

The Right Honourable Winston Churchill,
      10, Downing Street,
         London.

German forces invaded Russia on 22 June 1941. At first it seemed that Hitler
might sweep all before him, but the winter of 1941 halted the German spearheads
just short of Moscow and Leningrad. Churchill had always been hostile to
Communism, but he was also pragmatic and the priority of defeating Germany
over-rode all previous considerations – he commented privately that if Hitler
invaded Hell, he would find something favourable to say about the Devil in the
House of Commons. In practice, Churchill tended to distinguish between the
Soviet system, about which he said little, and the bravery of the Russian people.
Churchill's views of the Soviet regime did not change, but were set aside in view
of the need to work together. Even so, it took almost a year of negotiations

Opposite: The challenge facing
Churchill is shown in this map of the
territory controlled by the 'Axis Powers'
of Germany and Italy at the height of
their strength in 1942.
Map drawn by Cedric Knight

before an Anglo-Soviet Treaty professing long-term friendship was signed on
26 May 1942. The relationship with Russia was much less close than that with
the United States, and there were fewer face-to-face meetings. On these occasions
Churchill and Stalin had to communicate through interpreters, but even so a
working relationship was established on a basis of mutual respect. However, Stalin
was often suspicious of the closeness of the Anglo-American relationship, and
frequently had to be reassured that they would not leave Russia in the lurch.
Churchill called the wartime partnership of Britain, America and Russia 'the
Grand Alliance', and did his best to make it work. At the same time, he was aware
that the growth of Soviet power was likely to lead to problems in the future, and
he knew there was little that he could do to influence Stalin's actions. This was
particularly the case in the later stages of the war, as the Red Army pushed
German forces back and occupied the countries of east and central Europe.

At first, however, the crucial issue was saving Russia from collapse. Stalin
constantly pressed for an invasion of the European mainland that would draw
German forces away from Russia. However, any such 'second front' would have
to be a huge undertaking if it was to have a chance of success. In 1942 and 1943
Britain and America did not have the military strength, shipping or command
of the air necessary to land in France and assault the defences of Hitler's 'fortress
Europe'. Instead there were landings in Algeria in late 1942 and the invasion of
Sicily and Italy in 1943. However, although the latter diverted some German
troops, Stalin refused to accept these as effective second fronts, and he was bitterly
disappointed when the plan to invade France was postponed from 1943 to 1944.
In the absence of a second front, the only means by which Britain and America
could help was by bombing Germany from the air and supporting Russia with
aid and equipment. These were difficult to deliver, but as nothing else could be

done it was a priority to send much-needed war production to Russia via the perilous Arctic convoys or overland through Iran.

Britain's position was less perilous after Russia and the United States entered the war, but further setbacks in 1942 made this the lowest point for Churchill personally. British forces still seemed to be outnumbered and poorly equipped, and a series of military reverses in the first half of 1942 began to undermine confidence in Churchill's conduct of the war. Most damaging was the fall of Singapore in February 1942; British prestige in Asia was badly shaken, and within a few weeks Japanese forces were at the gates of India. Churchill diverted criticism with a reshuffle of the War Cabinet in February in which the rising Labour figure Stafford Cripps – popularly identified with support for Russia – was made Leader of the House of Commons. Cripps was not a success in this role and the chance that he might rival Churchill faded, but further setbacks in north Africa, culminating in the fall of Tobruk in June, led to another crisis. A vote of censure was moved by an obscure Conservative backbencher, Wardlaw-Milne, but the attack fizzled out in the debate on 1–2 July. Although there was concern about Churchill's dominance of decision-making, there was no real desire to replace him. Churchill made an effective reply, and the only serious parliamentary challenge of the war was comfortably defeated by 475 votes to 25.

Immediately after Pearl Harbor Churchill visited Washington in December 1941, and the strategy of 'Germany first' was agreed. The main debate was between preparing an invasion of northern Europe, which the Americans wanted but Churchill was dubious about, and his preferred focus on the Mediterranean. There were important British interests in this region, but Churchill's strategy was also based on the conviction that the enemy had a 'soft underbelly' which was vulnerable to attack. This had worrying parallels with Gallipoli, but a second visit to Washington in June 1942 secured agreement on the interim measure of a north African operation later that year. In August 1942 Churchill flew to Moscow where he met Stalin for the first time, and delivered personally the unwelcome news that the western Allies lacked the resources to attack in Europe that year, and would instead drive the enemy from north Africa. Churchill then flew to Egypt, where the setbacks had led to Wavell's successor, Auchinleck, being replaced by Alexander as overall commander, with Montgomery taking charge of the Eighth Army. This proved a winning combination, and with better resources at their disposal they prepared to counter-attack. The result was the decisive victory at El Alamein in November 1942, which drove Rommel's enemy forces back to Tunisia. Anglo-American forces also closed in from the west after the 'Operation Torch' landings in Algeria on 8 November, and by May 1943 the last hostile forces in north Africa had surrendered. El Alamein was a turning point in Britain's fortunes in the war, but Churchill was aware that there was still a long and difficult struggle ahead. Speaking at the Lord Mayor of London's annual banquet on 10 November 1942, he declared: 'This is not the end. It is not even the beginning of the end. But it is perhaps the end of the beginning.'

From late 1942 the flow of British and American war production began

M.O.S.T. S.E.C.R.E.T. T.E.L.E.G.R.A.M.

To- C. in C.Med.   From:-F.O."Z".

E M E R G E N C Y

Following received from Head of Italian Government begins:-

To, FRANKLIN D.ROOSEVELT, President of the U.S.A. and
WINSTON CHURCHILL, Prime Minister of Great Britain.

I thank you most warmly for the message which you, who direct
the destinies of such great Nations, have been pleased to send me,
in these hours so tragic for my country.

I place secure trust in your affirmation that the Anglo-
American Armed Forces who have already disembarked at various points
on the Italian Continent, will continue to pour in as numerous and
as eager to help, as the situation so imperiously demands.

Our own armed forces, already tested and scattered in Italy
and still more, outside Italy, cannot possibly unite and validly
oppose, alone, the German forces. But everything that is possible
is being and will be done with that same spirit and with that same
tenacity which we displayed together on the battlefields of Italy and
France during the last Great War.

I can assure you that the Italian People closely united
around their King, and longing at the cost of any sacrifice whatsoever
to achieve liberty and a peace with justice, will not fail manfully
to carry out on this occasion their duty - their whole duty. We
are not lacking in faith, and we will march with you, our American
and British friends.

(Signed) Marshal BADOGLIO.

to take effect, securing mastery in the air and increasing strength on the ground. There was still a long struggle ahead, but after victories in the Pacific, north Africa and at Stalingrad, it was clear that the tide was turning. The Anglo-American summit at Casablanca in January 1943 offered reassurance to Stalin by announcing the demand for the 'unconditional surrender' of Germany, but the continuing operations in north Africa made an attack in northern Europe increasingly unlikely in 1943. By May it was accepted that instead the Allied forces in north Africa would proceed to attack Sicily and open a second front in Italy. The plan for a cross-Channel invasion in May 1944 was finalised at another Anglo-American conference at Quebec in Canada on 9 August 1943, and the 'big three' of Churchill, Roosevelt and Stalin met for the first time at the Teheran conference of 28–30 November. Churchill celebrated his sixty-ninth birthday here with a reception at which Stalin toasted his health, and then travelled on to Tunis. However, he arrived unwell and exhausted, suffering from pneumonia and heart palpitations. He rested first at Eisenhower and Alexander's headquarters until Christmas, and on 27 December was flown to a villa at Marrakesh in Morocco to recuperate. Clementine joined him there, and he was well enough to return

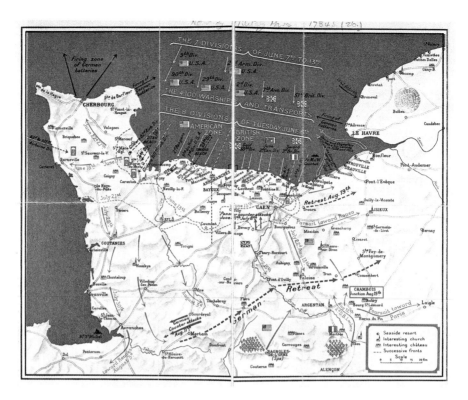

to Britain by battleship in mid-January. Although he recovered, his strength was less in the later stages of the war, and in the winter of 1944–45 he was becoming visibly exhausted.

On 5 June 1944 the Allies entered Rome, but the next day attention shifted to France with the 'D-day' landings on the Normandy beaches. As soon as possible afterwards, Churchill visited the beachheads on 12 June. The eventual breakout from Normandy was followed by a swift advance across France, with the liberation of Paris on 24 August. The thoughts of the Allied leaders were now turning to the shape of the post-war world, and in October 1944 Churchill visited Moscow for talks with Stalin. He accepted that he could do little for Poland, which was already effectively occupied by the Red Army, but he secured the 'percentages agreement' which divided the Balkans into spheres of influence. This gave Britain the dominant position in Greece and the eastern Mediterranean, and when civil war broke out in Greece between Communist forces and the provisional government in December 1944, Stalin honoured the agreement. To her distress, Churchill abandoned the family Christmas gathering which Clementine had laboured to arrange, and flew to Athens to try and bring both sides together. He had some success, but British forces had to intervene to suppress the Communist rising. The second and last gathering of the 'big three' leaders of the Grand Alliance was held at Yalta, in the Crimean peninsula, on 4–11 February 1945. This confirmed the

plans for the final offensives, the occupation policy for Germany and the establishment of the United Nations and its Security Council. Churchill had to accept Stalin's position over Poland, and was worried by Roosevelt's desire to deal directly with Stalin. However, the death of the US President a few weeks later on 12 April 1945 was a great blow to Churchill, who scarcely knew his successor, Harry Truman.

The crossing of the Rhine in March 1945 was followed by the final German collapse and, after Hitler's suicide, the remaining German forces surrendered on 7 May. The following day was proclaimed 'Victory in Europe' day; Churchill broadcast to the nation, and also appeared with the royal family on the balcony at Buckingham Palace – this was an unprecedented gesture, but one which acknowledged his role in the victory. It had been achieved at great cost,

Opposite: Churchill and (to the left)
Field Marshal Montgomery in the ruins
of the German citadel at Julich on
7 March 1945, as Allied forces crossed
the Rhine for the final offensives in
Germany.
Fred Ramage/Getty Images

not only in lives but in the exhausted state of Britain's finances and economy. The war also led to profound changes in Britain's position in the world: in November 1942 Churchill had declared 'I have not become the King's First Minister in order to preside over the liquidation of the British Empire', but there was little that he could do to prevent this. Traditional anti-colonialism and economic rivalry meant that the United States was hostile to Britain's imperial role, and this was the greatest area of disagreement between Churchill and Roosevelt. Economic weakness, the loss of prestige after the Japanese victories and stronger demands for self-determination had already led to significant concessions over India, paving the way to its independence in 1947. By the time of Churchill's death in 1965 almost all of the colonial possessions in Africa and elsewhere had gone, leaving Britain – as he had feared – no more than a minor European power.

This process of change was mirrored in domestic politics, where a new atmosphere of egalitarianism emerged in the period after Dunkirk. The belief that the war would produce a better society greatly benefited the Labour Party, which was seen as supporting the welfare proposals of the Beveridge Report of 1942. Churchill paid little attention to domestic policy and the home front was dominated by Labour ministers. There is no doubt that Churchill wanted most of all to succeed as a war leader, and he disliked anything which disrupted national unity or took attention away from the war effort – particularly party frictions and post-war planning. Churchill was comfortable with coalition, and not only in wartime; he always wished to broaden the government and form a ministry of all the talents. However, his neglect of the Conservative Party contributed to its wartime collapse, whilst Labour's popularity rose. Although some of their leaders were reluctant, the Labour Party left the Coalition after the German surrender, and on 23 May Churchill formed a 'caretaker government' to hold office until the

general election. Polling day was 5 July, but the results would not be announced until 26 July to allow the inclusion of the service votes from overseas. In the meantime Churchill attended the first sessions of the Potsdam peace conference, and whilst in Berlin visited the ruins of the Chancellery and Hitler's bunker.

Churchill was far from alone in misunderstanding the mood of the electorate and assuming that his prestige would sweep him back to power. However, although there was gratitude and admiration for his wartime role, to many he did not seem to have the qualities needed in a peacetime leader. The tone of Churchill's campaign was badly misjudged, in particular his first election broadcast on 4 June which suggested that a Socialist government would have to control public opinion by 'some form of Gestapo'. There was a lack of attractive policies and Churchill was too identified with the unpopular Conservatives. When the results were announced on 26 July the Labour Party had scored a landslide victory of 393 seats and the Conservatives were reduced to 213 – although not quite as bad as 1906, it was a shattering defeat. That evening Churchill went to Buckingham Palace and resigned as Prime Minister, and Labour took office under Clement Attlee. Churchill was now seventy years old, a statesman of world renown without a role.

Holding back the years 1945–1965

Churchill had assumed that he would win the general election, and was hurt by the unexpected rejection. There was a widespread feeling that it would have been better if he had bowed out at the moment of victory, instead of discarding the prestige of national saviour for the prosaic role of party politician. The problems of the post-war world were daunting, and Churchill was physically and mentally tired by the end of the war. As the election result became clear Clementine suggested that 'it may well be a blessing in disguise', to which her husband grunted 'at the moment it seems quite effectively disguised'. However, retirement held little appeal and Churchill spent the next decade striving to remain at the forefront of public life and world affairs. At first he was gloomy and irritable, and his mood was not helped by the difficult transition to ordinary life in the restricted circumstances of post-war Britain. The Churchills moved to 28 Hyde Park Gate and Clementine began the process of re-opening Chartwell; during the war more use had been made of the facilities of Chequers, the Prime Minister's official country house in Buckinghamshire. Churchill always found inactivity to be frustrating and depressing, and in this period he was difficult to cope with. There was friction with Sarah, tempestuous rows with Randolph and frequent 'scenes' with Clementine; the latter wrote to their youngest daughter Mary of 'our misery', telling her 'I'm finding life more than I can bear'. As before, these tensions were partly eased by periods of separation and travel abroad, which allowed Clementine a breathing space and reminded Winston of his dependence upon her.

In September 1945 Churchill accepted an invitation to stay in the luxurious villa at Lake Como in northern Italy which had been requisitioned by Field Marshal Alexander; Clementine was exhausted, and stayed at home. As Churchill relaxed and painted, his strength and interest began to revive. He then travelled

Previous page: Churchill in the
honorary uniform of an Air Commodore
of 615 Squadron, Royal Air Force: an oil
portrait by Douglas Chandor, 1946.
*National Portrait Gallery, Smithsonian
Institution/Art Resource, New York*

on to the French Riviera; as had been the case before the war, this was his
favourite destination and he was now more than ever the pampered and
honoured guest of his rich friends – in particular, often staying at Beaverbrook's
villa at Cap d'Ail. His restive spirit had always enjoyed travel, but it was not just
a change of scene that drew Churchill abroad during these years out of power.
In Britain his position was frustrating and the opportunities limited, for the size
of Labour's parliamentary majority meant that his efforts had little immediate
effect. Abroad, however, he was still a world statesman whose pronouncements
were regarded as significant. The invitations that he received to attend various
occasions as an honoured guest and speaker were attractive not just because all his
expenses were paid, but still more for the recognition and the chance to influence
international opinion.

The most famous example of this came during Churchill's next trip abroad,
when he visited the United States between January and March 1946. On 5 March
he spoke at Westminster College in Fulton, Missouri; this was a small campus, but
President Truman had a personal connection with it and accompanied him there.
The speech was broadcast throughout the United States, and Churchill caught
public attention with his declaration that 'From Stettin in the Baltic to Trieste
in the Adriatic, an iron curtain has descended across the continent'. Behind this,
in what Churchill termed 'the Soviet sphere', Moscow was exerting increasing
control. He warned that there was no limit to the expansionist aims of
Communism, and called for 'the fraternal association of the English-speaking
peoples' to co-operate for their mutual security. In America and Britain the
immediate reaction to the speech was hostile, as most of the public were weary of
conflict and unwilling to see the former ally as the new danger. Churchill seemed
to be out of step, but this time the knowledge that he had been right in the 1930s

made his warnings hard to ignore. The Fulton speech helped to shape opinion in senior American political and military circles, and it was a step towards the Truman Doctrine of 1947 and the Marshall Plan of 1948. Although this was not its first public use, the phrase 'iron curtain' stuck. When it became an increasingly visible reality with the tightening of Soviet control in the occupied countries during 1947–48 and the confrontation over the blockade of Berlin, Churchill's foresight once more seemed to be vindicated.

As the 'Cold War' developed, Churchill was often more interested in international issues than he was in domestic affairs. It was essential to strengthen relations with the United States and counter any tendency to isolationism, and Churchill believed that he could make a special contribution here. However, it was also vital that the free countries of western Europe should consolidate against the Soviet danger, and this would be impossible without Franco-German reconciliation. This was another bold step, and Churchill saw the means towards it in the movement for European unity that emerged on the continent after the war. In September 1946, at Zurich University in Switzerland, he advocated a Franco-German partnership and the creation of what became the Council of Europe, as steps towards 'a kind of United States of Europe'. His prestige was such that he was immediately seen as the leading figure in the European movement, and this was reinforced by further speeches at major events such as the Congress of Europe at The Hague in May 1948 and the first session of the Council of Europe at Strasbourg in 1949. He was introduced at the latter as 'the first citizen of Europe', which was true in terms of his fame but misleading as a description of his priorities. Churchill wanted to foster European co-operation, but from a detached position which would not diminish Britain's relationship with the United States and its links with the Empire and Commonwealth. When initiatives

Opposite: The statue of Churchill in
Paris, unveiled by Queen Elizabeth II
and the President of France, Jacques
Chirac, on the 80th anniversary of
the end of the First World War,
11 November 1998.
PA Photos

such as the Schuman plan for the integration of European coal and steel
industries emerged in the early 1950s, Churchill was unwilling to erode British
sovereignty and suspicious of the federalists' agenda of supra-nationalism and state
economic planning.

Before the war Churchill had habitually lived beyond his means, but his
post-war fame at last brought financial security. In November 1946 Chartwell
was purchased from him for £43,800 by a group of wealthy admirers led by
Lord Camrose, who then presented it to the National Trust on condition that the
Churchills should live there for the rest of their lives. This was a substantial capital
sum, but it was dwarfed by the money that he could now command for his
writing. Churchill was the only major wartime leader who was able or willing to
give his account of events, and he was already an accomplished author. To avoid
death duties and secure the benefits for the family, a trust was established which
owned the rights to his war memoirs, personal papers and the official biography
to be written after his death. In 1947 Camrose's *Daily Telegraph* Group paid the
huge sum of £550,000 for the war memoirs, of which £175,000 came to
Churchill directly and the remainder to the trust. The American market was
even more lucrative, with the book rights realising $250,000 and *Life* magazine
and the *New York Times* paying $1,150,000 for the serialisation. Churchill was
now wealthy, and he shortly afterwards purchased two farms which adjoined
Chartwell. Here he typically became involved in the livestock and market
gardening they produced, acquiring another hobby for the next decade, until
the farms were sold again in 1957.

The major undertaking of these years was his war memoirs, which he began
on his return from the United States in the spring of 1946. His working methods
were similar to before, with a team of research assistants to assemble the material

Opposite: Out of office after the Labour
victory in the 1945 general election,
Churchill spent much time travelling
abroad: he is seen here painting on the
shore of Lake Leman, Switzerland, in
August 1946.
Getty Images

and several secretaries to take dictation. However, this was on a larger scale, and
he drew on the help of General Ismay, Lord Cherwell, Sir Isaiah Berlin and
a range of senior wartime military and scientific figures. The six volumes of
The Second World War were published between 1948 and 1954, with the first two
volumes – *The Gathering Storm*, on the years up to 1940, and *Their Finest Hour*, on
the period of greatest danger – making the most impact. It appeared in the form
of a historical work, reproducing many of Churchill's memos and letters, but it
was far from objective. The first volume in particular reinforced the popular
condemnation of the appeasers of the 1930s, and depicted Churchill as more
consistent and clear-sighted than had really been the case. The detail and
documentation, together with Churchill's quality of language, made his account
seem persuasive and authoritative; he had not been joking when he observed that
history would vindicate him 'because I will write the history'. It reached a huge
audience, with an initial printing of the first volume of 200,000 copies in Britain
and 600,000 in the United States. The scale of his achievement was recognised by
the award of the Nobel Prize for Literature in October 1953, not long before the
appearance of the last volume, which dealt with the end of the Grand Alliance
and the foreshadowing of the Cold War to follow.

Churchill was still physically robust and generally in good health; a minor
stroke in August 1949, whilst staying with Beaverbrook on the Riviera, caused
some concern but had no lasting effect. He was determined to reverse the defeat
of 1945 and return to power, and did not see his age as a barrier. His absences in
the winter of 1945–46 and the confusion of command which followed produced
a critical reaction from the parliamentary party, but matters improved from early
1946 with Eden discharging the role of deputy leader. Churchill was still often
away from Westminster, travelling or working on his memoirs at Chartwell, but

he was usually present to give a lead on the important occasions. As he could strike out on his own initiative or use language that his colleagues thought intemperate, it was sometimes unclear whether it was his absence or his presence that gave rise to the greatest complaint. He spoke in the key debates in the House of Commons, at the Conservative Party's annual conferences, and at mass rallies such as the one held at Blenheim in August 1947. He chaired the periodic meetings of the shadow cabinet, but these were held as expansive lunches at Churchill's favourite venue, the Savoy Hotel, and were used mainly as an audience for his monologues. Whilst he kept control of the broad picture, detail and routine were delegated to others. His intermittent attendance remained an issue and, in view of his age, there were inevitably questions about whether he could or should continue. However, the Conservative rank and file did not wish to lose his leadership, and the MPs and shadow cabinet recognised that he could not be forced out. His prestige was too great, and he had no incentive to retire of his own accord.

The Labour government encountered increasing economic problems, and Churchill stepped up his attacks as the position worsened after 1947. He linked

Opposite: Churchill, with Clementine, campaigning at his constituency headquarters in Woodford, Essex, on 6 October 1951. He is giving the 'V for victory' sign that he had made famous during the war; the election resulted in his return to office for a second term as Prime Minister.
Getty Images

the hardships of shortages and ration cuts with irksome bureaucratic controls and the failure of Socialist nationalisation. He was more careful in opposing Labour's welfare measures, although support for the medical profession's resistance to the National Health Service took the Conservatives into dangerous waters. This remained a sensitive area and in 1949 Churchill made a further blunder, first threatening and then having to disavow a motion of censure on health policy. In general, his strategy was to concentrate on criticising the government, and wait for them to make mistakes and lose popularity.

Churchill was pragmatic about the changes which the Conservative Party needed to make in order to recover from defeat, and he made effective choices of personnel in the key areas. Eden was now clearly his heir apparent, although it was equally clear that he would have to bide his time until the old man chose to make way. As well as carrying the routine load as Churchill's deputy in the House of Commons, Eden did much to support the moderates and reformers in the party. In 1946 Churchill appointed Lord Woolton, a popular and effective wartime Minister of Food, to be Party Chairman. Although not previously a Conservative, Woolton was a striking success, and he raised substantial sums and revived the almost moribund local organisation. The development of policy was entrusted to the rising figure of R. A. Butler, who took charge of the Conservative Research Department. Churchill was concerned that too much activity in this area would give hostages to fortune and divert attention from the failures of the government, but demands within the party for a clear statement became too strong to resist. A committee under Butler prepared *The Industrial Charter* of May 1947, which accepted Labour's reforms and presented the Conservatives as moderate and in tune with the spirit of post-war Britain. Churchill was cool, considering it 'pink' and semi-Socialist, but he had never been reactionary or doctrinaire in domestic

affairs. He endorsed it, and its apparent success led to other similar statements.

Despite these efforts, the road back to power was slow and sometimes frustrating. The government's economic problems led to even more rigorous austerity measures, but there were no clear signs that the Conservatives were gaining ground. The failure to win back any seats in by-elections caused alarm, and Churchill faced an outburst of criticism from backbench MPs in March 1949. This soon faded with more promising results in the local government elections in April, and Churchill appeased the renewed demand for a statement of policy by authorising the publication of *The Right Road for Britain*, which became the party's manifesto. In September 1949 the Labour government was forced to devalue the pound, and in the general election of February 1950 the Conservatives gained eighty-eight seats. Labour held on to office, but their overall majority in the Commons was only six. There were now more opportunities for parliamentary opposition, and Churchill adopted a vigorous strategy of frequent censure debates and other procedural devices to delay bills and harry the government. At the annual party conference in October 1950 he endorsed the ambitious target of building 300,000 new houses a year, exploiting an area where Labour's record was vulnerable. The Labour cabinet were exhausted and divided, but when they called another election in October 1951 the result was still close. The Labour Party secured slightly more votes, but 321 Conservative MPs were elected and Churchill had a small but workable overall majority of 17.

Churchill became Prime Minister for the second time on 26 October 1951, a little more than a month before his seventy-seventh birthday. The government which he formed had strong echoes of the wartime Coalition, with posts for non-party figures such as Ismay and Cherwell, and an offer of merger to the Liberal Party. His own instincts and the narrowness of the victory ensured that the government followed a moderate line in home affairs. Labour's health and social security measures were fully funded, and the Conservatives demonstrated that they could successfully manage the economy using the new interventionist methods of Keynes. Almost all of the nationalizations remained in public ownership and only the last and most controversial cases – road haulage and the iron and steel industry – were reversed. R.A. Butler was a success as Chancellor of the Exchequer, and the government oversaw the removal of many restrictive controls and the welcome end of the wartime rationing system. Churchill wanted to avoid industrial conflicts and appointed Walter Monckton as Minister of Labour; he acted as a conciliator, and most disputes were resolved by negotiation and generous compromises. This was what the public wanted and the Conservative Party needed to escape from its negative pre-war image, but it has been criticised as encouraging the inflationary wage settlements which led to the economic problems of the following decades. Harold Macmillan was put in charge of the housing programme and achieved the target of 300,000 new homes, but the resources which were diverted to this added to the economic strains. As during the war, Churchill was happy with stability on the home front and the avoidance of risky or provocative measures. The moderate social and industrial policy and the acceptance of Labour's most significant changes seemed to narrow the ground between the two main parties, and suggested that a post-war 'consensus' had emerged.

Foreign affairs occupied Churchill's interest and concern much more than domestic matters. When he became Prime Minister, the Korean War was in its closing stages and the Cold War had become a worldwide confrontation. There were problems in Iran and over the agreed withdrawal from the Suez base in Egypt; Churchill was strongly opposed to this, but had to implement it in 1954.

Opposite: A few weeks after returning
to office as Prime Minister, Churchill
and Anthony Eden, his Foreign
Secretary and heir apparent, leave for
a visit to Paris, 17 December 1951.
Harold Clements/Getty Images

The problem of security in Europe remained but Britain was reluctant to join the proposed European Defence Community, which Churchill dismissed as 'a sludgy amalgam'. When this plan collapsed he successfully proposed instead the creation of the Western European Union, which involved no loss of sovereignty to a supra-national body, and the admittance of West Germany to NATO. Supporters of European unity had hoped for much more, but in fact Churchill's view had not changed: Britain 'should be with it though they could not be part of it'. The main reason for this was his vision of Britain's special role in world affairs, which would continue its influence despite relative decline. This was the concept – or conceit – that Britain had a unique position as the intersection of three separate circles, and so could link them together. Europe was one of the circles, but it would never be worth weakening the ties to the other two: the Empire (now becoming the Commonwealth), and the transatlantic partnership with the United States. The latter was of the greatest importance, and when General Eisenhower was elected President in November 1952 Churchill hoped to restore the wartime Anglo-American 'special relationship'.

Churchill also wanted to use his wartime prestige to seek détente with Russia, and his last great effort was a quest for international peace. He was horrified by the destructive power of atomic weapons and the danger they posed if the tensions of the Cold War should escalate. Russia had acquired the atom bomb in 1949; the first successful British test was in October 1952, but in the following month America developed the hydrogen bomb, a much more powerful weapon which raised the stakes again. Churchill hoped to bring Stalin to negotiations, but the Korean conflict blocked the way. However, Stalin's death on 5 March 1953 offered the possibility of a thaw in Soviet policy, and Churchill believed he could use his prestige to open communications with the new

leadership. On 11 May, without consulting the United States or his cabinet, Churchill made a speech in the Commons proposing a three-power summit. Eisenhower was reluctant, but agreed to a preliminary meeting of the western powers – enlarged to include France – to be held on the island of Bermuda in June. Churchill's stroke delayed the meeting until December, and little emerged from it; it neither moderated American suspicion of Russian intentions nor fostered a closer Anglo-American partnership. Churchill did not give up, and seemed to have more success in the following year. He secured an invitation to Washington in June 1954, where his reception reflected his personal standing rather than Britain's real influence. He stayed at the White House as Eisenhower's guest for three days, having every meal but one with the President; the exception was a lunch in his honour at the Capitol. Eisenhower was still sceptical, but now agreed to the idea of a summit in principle, and to Churchill's suggestion that a Russo-British meeting might pave the way. On his way home Churchill sent a telegram from the liner *Queen Elizabeth* proposing this, after a huge row with Eden who was strongly opposed. The cabinet were outraged at not being

Opposite: Queen Elizabeth II leaving
10 Downing Street after attending a
dinner on Churchill's last night as Prime
Minister, 4 April 1955; Sir Winston is
holding the door of her car, and behind
the Queen are Lady Churchill and the
Duke of Edinburgh.
Getty Images

consulted and forced Churchill to back down when it was discussed at the next meeting on 23 July, and the idea was abandoned when the Russians instead proposed an all-European conference. During the last months of his premiership Churchill still hankered after a meeting of leaders, but there was no more that he could do.

There had been a general expectation that Churchill would hold the premiership for a year or perhaps two and then hand over to Eden, who would have time to become established before the next election. In fact, Churchill stayed in office for forty-one months, frustrating Eden and exasperating his colleagues. His physical strength was failing but his determination had not diminished, and when needed he could summon up unexpected reserves and rise to the occasion. However, he had a minor stroke in February 1952 and a much more serious one in June 1953 which paralysed his left side and impaired his speech for two months, with a further two months of convalescence. He was fortunate that it happened just before the summer recess, and it was not reported in the press. Churchill would almost certainly have had to retire if Eden had not also been unwell following a botched operation in April 1953, but with his successor incapacitated for nearly six months the cabinet supported his remaining in office. Churchill's powers of resilience were shown in his remarkable recovery, and he was able to attend the Conservative Party conference at Margate in October and score a triumph with his speech. However, although there were some successes in the Commons as well, his performances were becoming erratic and his powers were clearly failing. In cabinet, he was more than ever given to long and rambling reminiscences which wearied his ministers. In March 1954 he told R.A. Butler: 'I feel like an aeroplane at the end of its flight, in the dusk, with the petrol running out, in search of a safe landing.'

When Eden returned in early 1954 Churchill hinted at retiring in June, but he continued to delay. On 14 June 1954 he was installed as a Knight of the Garter, becoming Sir Winston Churchill; then and later he refused the offer of a dukedom – the possible title being Duke of London – as he did not wish to leave the Commons or lose the name of Churchill. In October 1954 he had another triumph at the Conservative Party conference and carried through a reshuffle of cabinet posts, and he was in vigorous form at the celebrations of his eightieth birthday on 30 November. Both Houses of Parliament presented him with a portrait painted by Graham Sutherland, but Churchill detested it and it was destroyed by Clementine after his death. In early January 1955 Churchill at last acceded to the pressure, particularly from Macmillan, and fixed the start of the Easter recess as the date for his departure. His last speech in the House of Commons on 1 March was a carefully prepared review of world affairs, and suggested that the destructive power of nuclear weapons might lead to an era of peace through a balance of deterrence. In a special sign of recognition, Queen Elizabeth II and Prince Philip were his guests at 10 Downing Street for a farewell

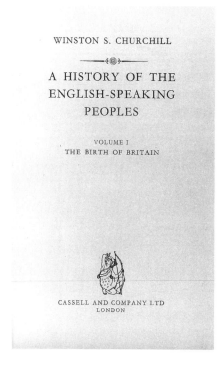

WINSTON S. CHURCHILL

A HISTORY OF THE
ENGLISH-SPEAKING
PEOPLES

VOLUME I
THE BIRTH OF BRITAIN

CASSELL AND COMPANY LTD
LONDON

Churchill's last great work was *A History of the English-Speaking Peoples*. Begun before the war, it was published in four volumes between 1956 and 1958.
The British Library, 9012 s9

dinner on 4 April 1955. On the next day he chaired his last cabinet, and in the afternoon resigned as Prime Minister.

In retirement, Churchill was often tired and depressed. He finished his *A History of the English-Speaking Peoples*, most of which had been written before 1939, and it was published in four volumes between 1956 and 1958. This was his last real literary work, and painting was the main relaxation of his later years, although for a while he was also interested in horse racing. He took longer vacations at the villas of various friends on the Riviera, and the Churchills celebrated their golden wedding anniversary here on 12 September 1958. From 1958 onwards, he took frequent cruises on Aristotle Onassis' yacht *Christina*. As time passed, he became more lethargic and withdrawn, sometimes lying in bed for much of the day. There were long silences, and time passed slowly for him; in 1959 he told Diana: 'My life is over, but it is not yet ended.' There were still some matters to resolve, including the plan to found a scientific and technical college at Cambridge University; Churchill College was opened in 1964, and his personal papers were later deposited there. In 1960, after considerable hesitation, he decided that Randolph would write his official biography; the choice made his son proud and brought them closer together. Randolph completed the first two volumes before his early death in 1968, after which it was continued in a further six volumes by Martin Gilbert.

Churchill had remained an MP and attended the Commons intermittently, although he did not speak; his last visit was on 27 July 1964, and he gave up his

The Churchill coin issued in the Isle of Man on the 50th anniversary of the end of the Second World War.
PA Photos

seat at the general election in October 1964. He had become very frail and now rarely spoke, but roused himself to wave to the crowds that gathered for his ninetieth birthday on 30 November 1964. A few weeks later, on 10 January 1965, he had a severe stroke, after which he was only semi-conscious. He lay in bed for two weeks, his strength declining, and died at 8.00 a.m. on Sunday 24 January, seventy years to the day after his father. Churchill was given a state funeral, the first for a commoner since the Duke of Wellington over a century before. His coffin lay in state for three days at Westminster Hall, during which over 300,000 people paid their respects. The funeral service at St Paul's Cathedral on 30 January followed instructions about the route and music which Churchill had earlier laid down. From St Paul's the coffin was taken by water to the Festival Hall, and then by train from Waterloo; he was buried next to his parents and brother in Bladon churchyard, within sight of Blenheim Palace.

Winston Churchill's political life spanned the first six decades of the twentieth century, and during almost all of this time he was one of the best-known and most significant of public men. He changed his party allegiance twice and was always suspected of being an ambitious adventurer, a diagnosis apparently confirmed by the political and strategic blunders which marked his progress. Churchill's career was unparalleled in its length and variety. It was marked by tireless endeavour, originality of mind, flawed judgements and remarkable achievements. Everything flowed from his extraordinary character and abilities, but his progress was continually hampered by the distrust which he aroused until

his wartime leadership in 1940. If he had retired from politics in the late 1930s, his career would certainly have outshone that of his father, but otherwise would have deserved the verdict of 'a study in failure'. Instead, he became the man of the hour in 1940. His leadership was of crucial importance after the fall of France, rallying the people behind the decision to fight on regardless. He was difficult to work for, but was also inspirational and energetic, producing a stream of ideas which were then filtered through his

immediate staff. The close relationship which he forged with President Roosevelt brought vital support for Britain in the darkest months of 1940–41, and he strove to maintain Britain's influence although its strength fell behind the emerging 'superpowers' as the war reached its close. Previously an opponent and a rebel, he was leader of the Conservative Party for almost fifteen years and oversaw its recovery of power in 1951, serving a second term as Prime Minister until 1955. He had always favoured a moderate and generous social policy, and helped the Conservatives to adjust and prosper in the changed atmosphere of the post-war era.

Churchill's stubborn and triumphant leadership in the Second World War was without doubt his greatest achievement. The 'finest hour' in 1940–1942, when total victory seemed to be almost within the grasp of Nazi Germany, determined the course not just of British but of world history. Much else in Churchill's career was bronze or even lead, but this was golden, and upon this alone rests his position as the most significant British figure of the twentieth century.

Chronology

1874	30 November: Born at Blenheim Palace, Oxfordshire
1888	April: Attends Harrow School
1893	September: Enters the Royal Military College at Sandhurst
1895	24 January: Death of his father, Lord Randolph Churchill
	February: Commissioned as a 2nd Lieutenant in the 4th Hussars, a cavalry regiment
1898	March: Publication of his first book, *The Story of the Malakand Field Force*
	2 September: Takes part in battle of Omdurman, near Khartoum
1899	July: Stands for Parliament in the Oldham by-election, but narrowly defeated
	November: Publication of *The River War*, a history of the reconquest of Sudan
	15 November: Captured by the Boers in the South African War
1900	1 October: Elected as Conservative MP for Oldham in the general election
1904	31 May: Leaves the Conservatives over Tariff Reform, and joins the Liberal Party
1905	10 December: First ministerial post as Under-Secretary for the Colonies in the Liberal government of Sir Henry Campbell-Bannerman
1906	January: Elected as Liberal MP for Manchester North-West and Life of his father, *Lord Randolph Churchill*, published to critical acclaim
1907	1 May: Privy Councillor, becoming the 'Right Honourable' Winston Churchill
1908	12 April: Enters the cabinet as President of the Board of Trade, but loses resulting by-election at Manchester North-West
	9 May: Finds new seat, elected as Liberal MP in by-election at Dundee
	12 September: Marriage to Clementine Hozier
1909	July: Birth of first child, Diana; two further surviving daughters born later, Sarah (1914) and Mary (1922)
1910	14 February: Appointed Home Secretary
1911	May: Birth of only son, Randolph
	24 October: Appointed First Lord of the Admiralty, responsible for the British navy
1914	26 July: Orders the fleet to its war stations; war declared on Germany on 3 August
	October: Attempts to organise the defence of Antwerp in Belgium
1915	April: British military landings on the Gallipoli peninsula in Turkey
	25 May: Demoted to Chancellor of the Duchy of Lancaster in the Coalition government formed by Asquith
	11 November: Resigns from the cabinet

1916	January–May: Military service, commanding a battalion on the Western Front
1917	17 July: Appointed Minister of Munitions in the Lloyd George Coalition government
1919	10 January: Returns to the cabinet as Secretary of State for War and Air
1921	15 February: Appointed Secretary of State for the Colonies
1922	September: Buys the Chartwell estate, near Westerham in Kent
	19 October: Out of office due to the fall of the Lloyd George Coalition
	15 November: Loses his seat at Dundee in the general election
1923	April: Publication of first volume of his history of the First World War, *The World Crisis*
	December: Defeated as Liberal candidate for Leicester West in the general election
1924	March: Stands as 'Constitutionalist' candidate in the Westminster Abbey by-election, but loses by 43 votes
	October: Returns to Parliament as MP for Epping, and rejoins Conservative Party
	6 November: Appointed Chancellor of the Exchequer by Baldwin
1925	April: Announces return to the gold standard in his first budget statement
1926	May: During the General Strike runs official newspaper, the *British Gazette*
1929	May: Conservative Party lose general election and Churchill leaves office
1930	October: Publishes the memoir *My Early Life*
1931	27 January: Resigns from Conservative 'shadow cabinet' over Baldwin's India policy
	August: Remains out of office when the National Government is formed
	31 December: Nearly killed in a traffic accident in New York
1933	March: Calls for increased spending on air defences
	October: Publication of first volume of *Marlborough*, biography of his famous ancestor
1934	June: Committee of Privileges rejects his accusation that the government has interfered in evidence submitted to the India Joint Select Committee
1936	7 December: Howled down in House of Commons during the abdication crisis
1939	3 September: War declared against Germany; Churchill returns to office as First Lord of the Admiralty

1940	10 May: Becomes Prime Minister in new Coalition, which includes Labour Party
	June: Broadcasts and speeches rally morale after the fall of France
	August: Start of Battle of Britain; speaks of debt owed to 'the few'
1941	June: Declares support for Russia after it is invaded by Hitler
	9–10 August: First meeting with Roosevelt at Placentia Bay, Newfoundland, and agreement on the 'Atlantic Charter'
1942	February: Fall of Singapore, Churchill reshuffles his government
	2 July: Wins vote of censure debate in House of Commons by 475 votes to 25
	November: Victory in battle of El Alamein in Egypt
1943	January: Churchill and Roosevelt confer at Casablanca
	November: Tehran meeting of 'big three': Churchill, Roosevelt and Stalin
1944	6 June: D-Day landings in Normandy
	9–10 October: Meeting with Stalin in Moscow, agreement on the Balkans
1945	4–11 February: Yalta conference of 'big three' leaders
	8 May: Victory in Europe day, after German unconditional surrender
	26 July: Churchill resigns as Prime Minister after Labour victory in general election
1946	5 March: 'Iron curtain' speech at Westminster College, Fulton, Missouri
1948	June: Publication of *The Gathering Storm*, first volume of *The Second World War*
1951	26 October: Becomes Prime Minister for the second time
1953	May: Churchill proposes a three-power summit, after the death of Stalin in March
	23 June: Suffers a serious stroke, which is kept secret from the media
	October: Awarded Nobel Prize for Literature
1954	14 June: Made a Knight of the Garter, becoming Sir Winston Churchill
	June: Visits Washington, guest of President Eisenhower at the White House
1955	5 April: Resigns as Prime Minister
1956	April: Publication of first volume of *A History of the English-Speaking Peoples*
1964	October: Retires from his seat in the House of Commons
1965	24 January: Dies at his home in London

Further reading

There are a great many books about Winston Churchill, of varying lengths and quality. The two best biographies of a reasonable length are:
Geoffrey Best, *Churchill: A Study in Greatness* (Hambledon and London, 2001)
Norman Rose, *Churchill: An Unruly Life* (Simon and Schuster, 1994)

Also useful is the longer biography:
Roy Jenkins, *Churchill* (Macmillan, 2001)

The eight volumes of the official biography, begun by Randolph Churchill and completed by Martin Gilbert, have been distilled by the latter into one summary work. This gives the fullest and most authoritative narrative:
Martin Gilbert, *Churchill: A Life* (Heinemann, 1991)

At the other end of the scale, there is a short and more analytical study:
Keith Robbins, *Churchill* (Longman, 1992)

Two of the most revealing books about Churchill are not conventional biographies, but studies of his political career:
Robert Rhodes James, *Churchill: A Study in Failure 1900–1939* (Weidenfeld & Nicolson, 1970)
Paul Addison, *Churchill on the Home Front 1900–1955* (Jonathan Cape, 1992)

There are two books which present different views of Churchill's approach to international issues before and during the Second World War. The first takes a controversial and critical stance, whilst the second is more favourable:
John Charmley, *Churchill: the End of Glory* (Hodder & Stoughton, 1993)
R.A.C. Parker, *Churchill and Appeasement* (Macmillan, 2000)

Finally, there is a substantial collection of essays which focus on many aspects of Churchill's life:
Robert Blake and W. Roger Louis, editors, *Churchill* (Oxford University Press, 1993)

Index